SUNSHINE STATE MAFIA

T0274968

UNIVERSITY PRESS OF FLORIDA

Florida A&M University, Tallahassee
Florida Atlantic University, Boca Raton
Florida Gulf Coast University, Ft. Myers
Florida International University, Miami
Florida State University, Tallahassee
New College of Florida, Sarasota
University of Central Florida, Orlando
University of Florida, Gainesville
University of North Florida, Jacksonville
University of South Florida, Tampa
University of West Florida, Pensacola

SUNSHINE STATE
MAFIA

A History of Florida's Mobsters, Hit Men, and Wise Guys

Doug Kelly

UNIVERSITY PRESS OF FLORIDA

Gainesville · Tallahassee · Tampa · Boca Raton
Pensacola · Orlando · Miami · Jacksonville · Ft. Myers · Sarasota

29 28 27 26 25 24   6 5 4 3 2 1

Library of Congress Cataloging-in-Publication Data
Names: Kelly, Doug, 1949– author.
Title: Sunshine State mafia : a history of Florida's mobsters, hit men, and
    wise guys / Doug Kelly.
Other titles: History of Florida's mobsters, hit men, and wise guys
Description: 1. | Gainesville : University Press of Florida, [2024] |
    Includes bibliographical references and index.
Identifiers: LCCN 2023037643 (print) | LCCN 2023037644 (ebook) | ISBN
    9780813080482 (paperback) | ISBN 9780813073224 (ebook)
Subjects: LCSH: Organized crime—Florida—History. |
    Mafia—Florida—History. | Gangsters—Florida—History. |
    Criminals—Florida—History. | BISAC: HISTORY / United States / State &
    Local / South (AL, AR, FL, GA, KY, LA, MS, NC, SC, TN, VA, WV) | TRUE
    CRIME / Organized Crime
Classification: LCC HV6452.F72 M348 2024 (print) | LCC HV6452.F72 (ebook)
    | DDC 364.109759—dc23/eng/20231107
LC record available at https://lccn.loc.gov/2023037643
LC ebook record available at https://lccn.loc.gov/2023037644

The University Press of Florida is the scholarly publishing agency for the State University System
of Florida, comprising Florida A&M University, Florida Atlantic University, Florida Gulf Coast
University, Florida International University, Florida State University, New College of Florida, University of Central Florida, University of Florida, University of North Florida, University of South
Florida, and University of West Florida.

University Press of Florida
2046 NE Waldo Road
Suite 2100
Gainesville, FL 32609
http://upress.ufl.edu

To the cops, prosecutors, politicians, jurors and judges
who refused to be bribed.

CONTENTS

PROLOGUE

It's a safe bet that my interest in Florida's infamous gangsters parallels yours. After I'd written three published books that have nothing to do with organized crime, for some reason the mystique of the Mafia flamed to the surface. It's as though fate grabbed me by the shoulders and said, "Write this book, Doug, and do it while you're still capable of typing."

Despite a spy novel near the completion stage, this compulsion forced me to focus instead on *Sunshine State Mafia*. Most existing material about the Mafia and organized crime in Florida over the past century understandably centers on South Florida and Tampa, but other cities have experienced various crime kingpins that merit a statewide picture between the covers of the same book.

You'll discover that *Sunshine State Mafia* is different from existing sources in that it's more than a reportorial account of notable mobsters. Indeed, my career as an international security consultant based at one time or another in Miami, the Florida Keys, and most recently Tampa Bay engendered personal brushes with several sundry characters. In addition, even despicable hit men and drug lords enjoy avocational pursuits, and my dual diversion as a fishing and golf writer sometimes put me together with real-life wise guys.

With one exception I never became friends with those on the wrong side of the law or knowingly worked for the bad guys against the good guys, although that can be tough to discern. Does a shoe salesman ask a customer what he or she does for a living? And even if one did, the answer wouldn't be, "I'm a gangster." Similarly, as the owner of a private investigative agency that provided services such as polygraph testing, mystery shopping, and technical surveillance countermeasures—locating clandestine bugs, telephone taps, hidden cameras and microphones—I accumulated a good many remarkable experiences, some of which are here revealed publicly for the first time.

It would be impossible between the covers of one book to depict every Mafioso who lived and did business in every portion of Florida, so I selected those I considered the most interesting and impactful. *Sunshine State Mafia* is based on myriad sources with added anecdotes from my experiences.

Why another book on the Mafia? For one thing, it's a rendition encompassing the entire state and doesn't focus on any one city or area. Many excellent books go into great detail about organized crime figures in Miami and Tampa, and they're highly recommended reading—being historical in nature, they still earn shelf life even if published many years ago. Not relying just on what's been written previously, I can't even estimate all the emails and phone calls involved or the amount of time spent examining governmental and law enforcement reports with the objective of making *Sunshine State Mafia* read like a *Reader's Digest* of selected mobsters. Fortunately, research that used to take months and even years to compile and required visits to libraries, historical societies, court houses and law enforcement offices can now be largely accomplished digitally.

I've organized the book as a geographical swing around the state to depict many of the colorful characters involved in organized crime. We'll kick it off in South Florida—the Keys, Miami, Fort Lauderdale, Palm Beach—then go to the southwestern portion of the state—Everglades City, Naples, and Fort Myers—and then swing through Central Florida—Orlando and Tampa—moving on to the north and northeast, from Jacksonville to Pensacola.

There's nothing in *Sunshine State Mafia* incriminating anyone. I'm also highly cognizant of personal safety, so I'm not going to "uncover" crimes that haven't been previously exposed or that might put someone in prison. Remember, we're not dealing here with members of the Boy Scouts of America. Nonetheless, many of those who served time in prison and/or testified in exchange for lighter sentences have come forward on YouTube channels with very compelling renditions of their crimes and misdeeds. If you haven't done so already, check them out.

I intended to put together a Mafia tour at the end of chapters on some cities. The driving maps would include former Mafia residences, favorite gathering places such as hotels and restaurants, and front companies used to wash money. However, an attorney friend advised that doing so would inevitably invite litigation by those whose homes or properties are no longer connected to organized crime. That seems an unlikely scenario, and in most cases we could "get away with it" by staying on public access sidewalks and streets. However, drawing the ire of Mafiosi or innocent citizens and business owners isn't in my wheelhouse, plus many of those locations don't exist anymore, having been demolished or replaced by entirely new structures. Nonetheless, the chapters do include many of the residence addresses of past mobsters, if your curiosity demands to know, and the "Mafiosi Domiciles" section at the back of the book gives additional addresses. Having said that, the walking tour of Ybor City in Tampa operated by Scott Deitche (pronounced "ditchy"), the author of many books on Tampa Bay's Mafia history, is outstanding—visit tampamafia.com.

Thanks for joining me on what's been a wild ride through the lore of Florida's gangsters, hit men, drug lords and other bad apples chronicled in *Sunshine State Mafia*.

1

MAFIA 101

Mafia junkies—you and me included—have lots of company. People's fascination with the malevolent world of American criminals starts with Old West legends such as Billy the Kid, Jesse James, and Butch Cassidy and the Sundance Kid. That segues to infamous mobsters of the early twentieth century: Al Capone, Lucky Luciano, Meyer Lansky and Vito Genovese. A later generation brought us Frank Costello, Paul Castellano, Sam Giancana and John Gotti. And though law enforcement continues to crack down on the Mafia and organized crime, it still exists and probably always will at some level.

Does that fascination make us tolerant of those who engage in murders, extortion, racketeering, drug dealing and the like? Of course not. We're simply intrigued by it all, which is why movies and novels like *The Godfather, Goodfellas* and *Casino* became blockbusters. The internet features ex-Mafiosi (the plural of Mafioso) who turned state's evidence or got convicted and are now out of prison recounting their criminal deeds, of course stopping just short of incriminating themselves for any crimes not divulged that could put them back in prison.

What exactly defines the Mafia as opposed to organized crime? The answer is that a Mafia is an organized crime "family" with a ranking of its members and composed of a particular ethnicity. The most infamous and powerful has been the Italian Mafia, with most original members hailing from Sicily. It is also known as *La Cosa Nostra*—"This thing of ours" in Italian—and only those with Italian ancestry can become "made" members of Mafia families. Often the *La* is dropped and just *Cosa Nostra* referenced. All others of various descents can associate and collaborate with the Mafia but cannot be a made member, as in the cases of Meyer Lansky (Jewish) and Henry Hill (Irish).

While the Italian Mafia in America is the best known—one can be from any part of Italy—other Mafia nationalities exist, such as Irish, Mexican, Russian and Cuban. "Mafioso" and "wise guy" are terms defining a Mafia member, whereas a mobster or gangster more aptly refers to anyone who's chosen to make a living on the wrong side of the law. All Italian Mafia families essentially consist of the same order of authority, and although the total number of members per family varies, it historically varied between 200 and 400 (nowadays only a fraction of those numbers exist per family, as is discussed later).

Organized crime can be simply classified as two or more conspirators who commit crimes. Two people holding up a store constitute an organized effort if one serves as the lookout and the other performs the stickup. Organizations of criminals can number in the dozens or even hundreds if involved in a large-scale drug cartel composed of growers, lab workers/processors, transporters (often called "mules"), city/regional distributors, and street dealers.

Sometimes there's a merging of interests when large sums of money are at stake, whereupon the Mafia works with other organized groups, such as drug cartels, other ethnic Mafiosi, or gangs.

It's believed that original members of *Cosa Nostra* emigrated from Sicily to New Orleans. It has been reported that Joseph Macheca organized a Sicilian gang there as early as 1868. In ensuing years, members drifted to other American cities—mostly to New York City but also handfuls to cities north of New Orleans as well as to Tampa. In Italy there exist four active Mafia groups: 'Ndrangheta, Sacra Corona Unita, Camorra and the Sicilian Cosa Nostra.

There are still remnants of five NYC Mafia families: Colombo, Bonanno, Genovese, Gambino and Lucchese. In Chicago it's called The Outfit, and so on, with families in Philadelphia, Buffalo, Los Angeles, Boston, etc. As the years progressed, Florida cities began to host Mafiosi and their illegal activities, which we'll chronicle in *Sunshine State Mafia*. Tampa had the most defined Mafia family in Florida, beginning with Ignacio Antinori and Santo Trafficante Sr. and Jr. Non-Italian and native Tampan Charlie Wall also hugely impacted organized crime in Tampa in the early part of the twentieth century.

Let's now go over the titles and ranks that compose a Mafia family:

Boss—Sometimes referred to as the Don, he oversees all those below him in the family in the manner of a company's board chairman. All the members of the top echelon report to him and carry out his orders. Bosses derive income from their family's criminal enterprises as well as percentages from other families. People complaining about, or questioning, the authority of their family's boss do so at their own peril.

MAFIA FAMILY

ORGANIZATIONAL CHART

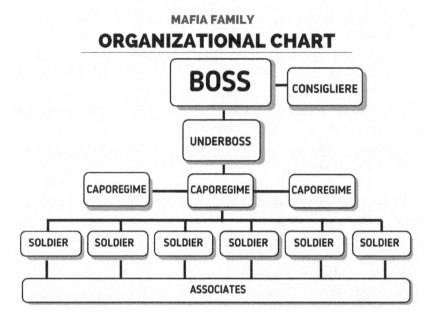

A Mafia family is a structured organization with strict levels of authority. (Chart created by Kelly S. Kelly)

Underboss—The #2 man in the family. His role is more like that of a hands-on CEO, communicating often with capos and soldiers. He's viewed as the likely successor to the boss and is expected to carry out his orders without question. In the pursuit of loyalty and to lessen the odds of being murdered by an ambitious underboss, the boss often chose an underboss related to him or a trusted long-term ally.

Consigliere—Pronounced "con-sig-lee-air-ay," he's the boss's personal consultant who can provide advice with significant decision-making. He can be an old-timer with a sense of *Cosa Nostra* history and connections or one whose opinion the boss trusts and respects. He's often a mediator of internal family squabbles and can represent the boss at meetings. The boss, underboss and consigliere form the decision-making triad of a family, known as the "administration."

Capo—Short for caporegime. He's similar to a captain in the military, but in this case also considered a street boss. A capo directly oversees a crew, known as a regime. A family typically has several capos, each with crews composed of soldiers and/or associates. Capos are chosen by the boss or underboss, and each capo pays them a cut of whatever the crew earns from loansharking, gambling, prostitution, thefts, burglaries, extortion, insurance fraud and other crimes perpetrated in their territories.

Soldier—As the name suggests, a soldier is a crewmember who obeys his capo's orders and is more of a street operative. To become a soldier, one must be a made man. Although the low man on the family totem pole of made men, a soldier is nonetheless a respected Mafia member and it can become a segue to upward mobility in a family. Soldiers must check with their capos several times a week to report everything they're doing, whether legitimately or illegally, an important process known as "putting it on record." Soldiers can be earners and/or enforcers.

Associate—This is a crew member who is not a made man due to his heritage not being Italian, or to not being nominated or not being fully trusted. The latter could be due to having a past involving law enforcement or an unfavorable reputation. Examples of famed associates in the Lucchese family in the 1970s and '80s portrayed in the movie *Goodfellas* were Henry Hill and Jimmy Burke, both being of part Irish descent and therefore ineligible to become made members. Those "in the life" of *Cosa Nostra* sometimes refer to associates as "civilians" and made men as "friends."

A made man is therefore someone of Italian descent who rose through the ranks as an associate or crew member. Originally both parents of a made man in the U.S. *Cosa Nostra* had to be not only of Italian descent but also only from Sicily. Since that eventually proved too restrictive, descent can be from any part of Italy, but the requirements have swung back and forth that at least one family member must be of Italian descent, and then at least the father must be Italian.

It has become more difficult to be a made man due to increased use of wiretaps and informants by the FBI and prosecutors. If a Mafioso recruits someone who turns out to be an informant, the penalty is death. The advent of the Racketeer Influenced and Corrupt Organizations (RICO) Act in 1963 and the Organized Crime Control Act of 1970 broadened the definition of crimes and imposed harsher penalties for racketeering, allowing for prosecutors to file charges that stick and to increase prison terms. Sentences for crimes involving illegal drugs became significantly more severe as law enforcement recognized how lucrative the drug trade became for drug traffickers and the Mafia, especially after Prohibition ended in 1933 and casino gambling operations were shut down.

Consequently, it has become more dangerous to recruit a family member. Worse yet, the specter of long prison terms caused some Mafiosi when under prosecution to break the code of *omerta*—the swearing of secrecy when becoming a made man. Adding to the frequency of members becoming informants or rats, RICO seizures of assets often leave their loved ones destitute. When a mob member makes a deal to testify for the government, he and his family will usually be targeted for death to silence them unless they can be put into the Federal Witness Protection Program. Nowadays, many ex-Mafiosi who cooperated and served sentences not only escaped the wrath of the mob but have become successful internet hosts regaling their past hits and illegal activities—but they wisely mention only crimes they've already divulged on record.

As already stated, to become made initially required both the mother and father to be Italian, but that gave way to just the father being a full-blooded Italian. Originally, only one made man was required as a sponsor, but now two or more are required, of which at least one must have known the proposed man for at least 10 years. The necessity to go to two or more sponsors represents a countermeasure to lessen the chance of infiltrating the *Cosa Nostra,* as former FBI agent Joe Pistone did so spectacularly for five years, posing as jewelry expert Donnie Brasco. When a family is interested in adding a made man, it's known as being "open book" time; conversely, it's "closed book" when not interested.

The induction for a made man to be fully initiated takes place in a baptism-like ceremony in a secluded location. Surrounded by sponsors and usually in the presence of the boss of that family, the candidate (or candidates) "earns his badge" by swearing to *omerta,* the Mafia code of silence. With a pistol and knife resting on a nearby table, his trigger finger is punctured so that drops of blood drip onto a picture of a saint. An edge of the picture is set on fire and he moves it from hand to hand as it burns his palms while he repeats an allegiance to *Cosa Nostra* spoken by one of those at the ceremony. Often there's an informal social gathering afterward. In most cases, either earlier, while an associate, or soon, for a newly made man, he must commit a murder ordered by his boss to prove his willingness to carry out orders and to confirm that he is not a member of law enforcement.

All non-associate members of a family are made men and as such must be respected among all those in *Cosa Nostra* and cannot be harmed by other mobsters. The only exception to the untouchable rule is if the leaders of a family give such permission, which usually must come from the family's administration and be agreed to by the Commission. An intention to harm or kill a made member must be given during a sit down whereby the grievance is voiced. Only if all parties to the sit down arrive at a consensus will any action take place. Failure to obtain such approval often results in death to the perpetrator.

Be sure to refer to the glossary toward the back of the book for a comprehensive and up-to-date set of definitions and Mafia-speak.

The Mafia also established rules for all family members, and each family adopted an individual code within the rules for ethics and behavior. Some breached the rules or codes, but most did not for fear of reprisal. These rules or codes include only approaching another made man when introduced by a fellow made man, not hitting on the wife and/or girlfriend of a wise guy, and making yourself available 24/7 for Mafia business.

Any relationship with a cop is forbidden, even if indirectly through a friend or relative. Even being seen with a cop is a no-no. If a wise guy spots another wise guy talking with a cop, it immediately raises suspicion that he's a CI—a confidential informant. Family members are advised to avoid unwanted attention by staying out of lawsuits and other legal entanglements unless counter suing. Keeping a low profile by not being flashy or seeking publicity has long been the norm, although some gangsters seemed to enjoy the limelight, such as Capone and Gotti—both of whom ended up as federal targets and imprisoned (Gotti died in prison; Capone served nine months for one conviction and over seven years for another).

From its inception until the 1980s, any member of a Mafia family involved in illegal drugs would risk being killed on sight by another Mafioso without the usual requirement of a sit down. This policy was reinstated in the mid-1980s by Gambino boss Paul "Big Paulie" Castellano and Genovese underboss at the time Vincent "The Chin" Gigante. The Mafia disdained involvement in illegal drugs because the drugs' habit-forming effects can cause someone to draw heat. Some wise guys privately violated that rule, but not many. In addition, it cannot be overstated that the ever-increasing harsh prison terms for those caught dealing drugs provided a growing incentive to cooperate with prosecutors.

However, the anti-drug mentality has changed greatly since the 1980s for two reasons: The Mafia could no longer ignore the enormous earning potential of illegal drugs, and other traditional forms of income from illegal activities were shrinking, partly due to broader forms of prosecutions because of the RICO Act.

Earners, it must be stressed, are the lifeblood of a family, providing income streams via all forms of crimes. Often the portrayals of hit men in fictionalized accounts are thug-like and uneducated, but that's seldom the case. In fact, a successful hit man (see glossary) working alone or in a team must be well organized and a good planner to commit murders and get away with them.

Let's start wading into the weeds of how the Mafia took hold in America, how it spread into Florida, and some of the controversial wise guys who did business there.

2

A GIFT FROM UNCLE SAM

Who's to blame for the rise of the American *Cosa Nostra?* Sadly, the fuel for the fire that sprung five New York City Mafia families and families in other cities like Tampa involved a successful puritan movement to rid America of the production, sale or transportation of alcohol. Known as the National Prohibition Act, it went into effect in 1920 and dragged on until its repeal in 1933. Exceptions were made for medicinal uses and, ironically, for some religions. People could mix booze for personal consumption, but that didn't satisfy the thirst of the masses.

After World War I, one of the nation's most divisive issues was whether one was "dry" or "wet." Without going into page after page of soggy details, here's a snapshot of Prohibition from beginning to end, because it's so crucial to the birth of the Mafia.

Many temperance and religious groups feverishly backed banning alcohol, and they soon wielded major clout with members of Congress, in both the House and Senate. Those groups were loud and well-funded, and they organized humongous protest marches that fetched massive newspaper coverage—which quickly got the attention of politicians, who live off votes.

But then, as now, the media could sometimes sway public opinion in the wrong direction. Accordingly, Congress badly misjudged the will of the people and for over a decade lacked the foresight of the vehement pushback that came. And so, initially scared by the threat of losing their seats, congressmen drafted the National Prohibition Act in 1917 and passed it on January 19, 1919, as Amendment 18 to the U.S. Constitution. That had required two-thirds of Congress and three-fourths of what were then 48 states to ratify it. All but two states did ratify it, with only Rhode Island and Connecticut saying no.

After realizing the law possessed little in the way of teeth for enforcement, Congress passed the Volstead Prohibition Enforcement Act on October 28, 1919. That gave the Commissioner of the IRS in the U.S. Department of the Treasury the legal authority to create a Prohibition Unit.

Theo Proctor in Tallahassee driving an automobile in support of Prohibition, sometime before 1920. Those campaigning for Prohibition were known as "dry" and those against making alcohol production and consumption illegal as "wet." (floridamemory.com)

You will recognize the name Eliot Ness, a Prohibition agent extraordinaire based in Chicago.

The National Prohibition Act, also known as the Volstead Act, became law on January 17, 1920, but not without some presidential fireworks. Only the Senate and House can pass amendments to the Constitution, but the Volstead Act required that it be signed into law by President Woodrow Wilson—and he vetoed it. However, the Senate and House overrode the veto. The next three presidents—Harding, Coolidge and Hoover—were against Prohibition but lacked the votes in Congress to repeal it. That changed when President Franklin Roosevelt—and a nation badly divided, with organized crime now out of control—finally succeeded in overseeing passage of Amendment 21, which repealed Amendment 18 on December 5, 1933. It was the one and only time in American history that an amendment was repealed.

But like the boxer who drops his guard and gets KO'd, 13 years of Prohibition proved to be a bloody affair when it came to the rise of *Cosa Nostra* and myriad bootleggers. No beer, no rum, no vodka? Wrong. That just never set well with a public historically fond of partying, and they were not going to be denied. Illegal stills sprang up, underground speakeasies in the tens of thousands drew huge crowds—you just gained entry at the door by giving the correct password through the infamous sliding peephole. Booze poured in faster than the feds could smash the endless kegs of beer and mountainous cartons of bottles. While small-time bootleggers pocketed lots of cash, fellows like Lucky Luciano and Al Capone—and non-Mafia

Illegal stills sprang up in rural areas of Florida during Prohibition, which were destroyed when found by law enforcement. (floridamemory.com)

entrepreneurs like Joe Kennedy—recognized that an organized effort would direct millions into their pockets.

Prohibition ultimately crashed, never to be forgotten. When the curtain finally dropped in 1933, banners went up saying, "Happy days are beer again." But during that 13-year dry span, the opportunity to fulfill the void became as fortuitous as Willy Wonka's golden tickets. Some small-time street thugs became big-time street thugs. As mentioned in chapter 1, five NYC crime families soon emerged and took advantage of Prohibition in a big way. With the influx of bootlegging cash came the presence of sizable bribe money. Men whose last names ended in vowels, who drove fancy cars and sported expensive suits, garnered power and respect on the streets.

The most ambitious of the criminal element put together bootlegging operations that—like a legitimate corporation—required an organization in order to maximize profits. A boss, managers, and a staff to carry out the duties took shape, but unlike other endeavors bound by government rules, laws, and licenses, the Mafia could operate behind the cover of legit businesses while illegally making tax-free money hand over fist.

As the illegal industry of bootlegging began to explode, so did the "discovery" of Florida. A subtropical state possessing the exclusivity of an Atlantic coastline and a Gulf of Mexico coastline represented phenomenal potential. Henry Flagler's railroads connected populated sections of the state, and roads were being paved everywhere. Marinas sprang up to host a boom in boat construction, and soon came the blossoming of residential housing and development of hotels. Entrepreneurs like Julia Tuttle—the

"Mother of Miami"—and Henry Plant in Tampa recognized the enormous appeal of year-round sunshine and spectacular beaches.

People began coming, first to visit, then to live. Novelists Zane Grey and Ernest Hemingway helped publicize Florida's fishing bounty; naturalists like Marjory Stoneman Douglas extolled the distinctive beauty of vast swamps teeming with wildlife. A land boom began in the 1920s and expanded despite occasional hurricanes. Meanwhile, as Prohibition ended in 1933 and the Depression waned with Franklin Roosevelt's New Deal setting recovery in motion, World War II found America emerging from the hell of war as the world's dominant economic and military power. And Florida, with its sunshine, picturesque coastlines, alligators, and flamingos, began attracting tourists from all over the country—including wise guys.

The Sunshine State offered something even juicier than warm weather: little or no law enforcement. Crooks already existed in Florida, but the entire state represented virgin territory for organized crime. Mafiosi experienced at setting up front companies and washing money could move in and immediately take over criminal activities. They also mastered the art of bribery, and the sad reality is that the temptation of pocketing a couple of C-notes often proved too much to pass up for cops squeaking by on 20 bucks a week. The same applied with prosecutors, judges and politicians, who could easily turn a blind eye or a friendly wink—or even brazenly aid and abet well-heeled mobsters.

From Jacksonville to Key West to Pensacola and all points in between, lax law enforcement and a naïve justice system offered little or no resistance to the influx of crime members who became part- or full-time residents while setting up illegal operations. After World War II the mob became involved in gambling, prostitution, extortion, robberies and drug trafficking. They started or took over legit businesses like hotels and restaurants, using many to launder cash. Florida began serving as a base for Mafia enterprises and activities in the Caribbean, Bahamas, and Central and South America.

Although a Bureau of Investigations (BI) came about in 1908 under the auspices of U.S. Attorney General Charles Bonaparte—grandson of famed French General Napoleon Bonaparte—it didn't have the resources to fight the surge of crime and corruption. Eliot Ness etched his name in the history books in Chicago by enforcing Prohibition and harassing Al Capone. J. Edgar Hoover was appointed BI director in 1924 during Prohibition, and 11 years later emerged as director of the present-day FBI, a position he occupied until his death in 1972. Hoover did receive the resources in terms of personnel and budget and equipment to become a serious force, but for most of Hoover's tenure he focused on outing communist spies and tracking left-wingers, and at one point was actually quoted as saying there was no such thing as the Mafia.

In 1950–51 Congress began pressuring the Mafia with the famed Kefauver Committee chaired by U.S. Senator Estes Kefauver from Tennessee. His committee held hearings in 14 cities and interviewed over 600 suspected members of organized crime. Most mobsters famously pleaded the fifth, but a few did testify, and it became clear that the Mafia was real and much larger in scope than most people realized. U.S. Attorney General Bobby Kennedy came along in the early 1960s and became a thorn in the side of mobsters such as Chicago boss Sam Giancana. As U.S. Attorney for the Southern District of New York, Rudy Giuliani gave mob bosses hell in the 1980s.

Sunshine State Mafia isn't mainly about the good guys, although they do get a chapter at the end of the book. And while many of the old-time mobsters who didn't get whacked ended up in the slammer, most of them hired well-connected attorneys and beat the raps. More often than not in Florida, any punishment meted out for underworld activities resulted in little more than a slap on the wrist, or outright freedom, thanks to prosecutors and judges on the take.

Now, turn the page and let's highlight some of the wise guys who garnered a fondness for suntans.

3

CALAMITIES IN THE KEYS

If your last name was Farto, would you want people nicknaming you Bum? Evidently Joseph "Bum" Farto didn't mind it a bit, and that alone probably hints at his being a person of interest.

Born in 1919 across the street from the Key West Fire Department, Bum Farto hired on as a fireman in the 1940s and worked his way through the ranks until becoming the fire chief in 1964. Fate handed him that job thanks to a long tenure and an FBI investigation into corruption in both the island's fire and police departments, the result of which entailed the resignation of then Fire Chief Charles Cremata and Police Chief George Gomez. Combined with a new police chief, Farto gave rise to hopes by the island's residents that he would clean things up and restore order in the all-important fire department—most of Key West's structures were made of wood.

But that was a tall order. The already shaky reputation of Key West— referred to by some as Key Weird—as a bawdy, open town began in the late 1800s when the main business activity centered on salvaging wrecks. Suspicions ran high as to whether the wrecking crews in shallow-draft boats purposely misdirected large ships laden with goods onto jagged reefs. Many other wooden keels fell victim to faulty charts that misplaced reefs or lighthouses that often would mysteriously go dark on stormy nights.

Although the Florida Keys consist of about 1,700 islands (keys), only 43 are connected south of the state's mainland, from Key Largo to Key West via the bridges of U.S. Highway 1 that separates the Atlantic Ocean, Florida Bay and the Gulf of Mexico. Monroe County, the southernmost county in Florida, envelopes all of the Florida Keys and portions of Everglades National Park and the Big Cypress National Preserve. Since 1990 the entirety of the Keys and surrounding waters lie within a national marine sanctuary. Key West received national notoriety when Ernest Hemingway decided that the southernmost city suited him just fine. The novelist lived there in the 1930s, allocating plenty of time when not writing or fishing to haunt-

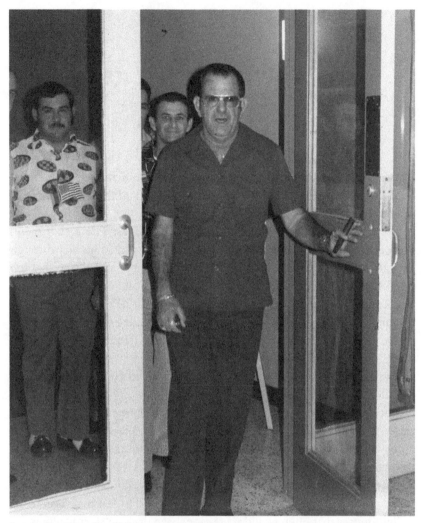

Former Key West Fire Chief Joseph "Bum" Farto heads out the door with cigar in hand, circa 1970. He went on the lam after a drug conviction and his fate is still a mystery. (Monroe County Public Libraries, Florida Keys History Center, Online Digital Collection)

ing Duval Street's sordid watering holes and brothels. Key West became a clique of fishermen, rum guzzlers, and folks who didn't care much for outsiders meddling in their affairs.

Nonetheless, by the 1950s word reached Florida's capital city of Tallahassee that things smelled fishy in Key West, which by then had attracted all kinds of residents with liberal drinking habits and questionable character.

The island became a frequent hangout for Fulgencio Batista, the Cuban dictator who, the feds knew, was playing ball with the Mafia. Even his future nemesis, Fidel Castro, dropped by the city to bask in capitalist-style leisure before he took to the mountains of Cuba to orchestrate a communist takeover.

Besides part ownerships and investments in Havana casino hotels and other coastal resorts lying a mere 90 miles south of Key West, the Mafia operated with total impunity in Cuba, the Pearl of the Antilles. Reciprocally, Cuba became a Mafia business partner completely outside the reach of the U.S. government, and it didn't take a Sherlock Holmes to recognize that this could not occur without complicity and total cooperation on the part of Batista. And the dictator sure wasn't doing it for free.

The Cuba-Mafia connection ran deep in Key West. Tampa Mafia boss Santo Trafficante Jr., who inherited from his dad a bolita operation in Tampa, Orlando, Miami, Key West and later Cuba, undoubtedly crossed paths with Batista if not one of his henchmen. The common denominator: The popularity among the Latin community of bolita, which gained traction in the 1880s in Tampa and was enhanced in the 1920s by then Tampa mob boss Charlie Wall (for more about Wall see chapter 15).

Bolita involves an illegal form of gambling often referred to as a "numbers game." It's a daily game in which 100 numbered balls are placed into a bag, the bag is shaken a few times, and one of the balls is blindly drawn. If your ball gets picked, you win a portion of the money pooled and the rest goes to the sponsor—in this case, the Mafia. Although most individual bets are usually a dollar or less, the simplicity of it adds to the popularity and thus can enrich the winners and bring in a steady daily cash flow to the mob. Like all forms of gambling, it can be rigged in a variety of ways. The progression here is that keeping up the flow of illegal bolita money involves making sure palms get greased, and thus the corruption element also comes into play with law enforcement and the legal system.

But essentially Batista made himself the legal system in Cuba, and he fed at the Mafia trough. Although Santo Trafficante Sr. died in 1954, as already mentioned his son—Luigi Santo Trafficante Jr.—inherited control of organized crime in Tampa with partnerships in Cuba and South Florida. Through the Trafficante connections and coordination of organized crime with Mafia families in New York City and New Orleans, business in Cuba flourished under the protection of Batista's dictatorship. And hence all other aspects of Mafia dealings besides bolita sprouted openly in Cuba and also in Florida: casino skimming, prostitution, extortion, loan sharking, insurance fraud, and with it numerous corrupted officials. Those who tried to stand in the way quite often disappeared when fishing or on Everglades hunting trips.

In the late 1950s heroin became of interest to the Trafficantes, even though the NYC families—still controlled by old-school *La Cosa Nostra* bosses—eschewed it. A perfect conduit for heroin and later other narcotics into the U.S. involved Havana serving as the hemisphere's distribution center. After Cuba received flights and shipments from various countries like Colombia and Turkey, speedboats had their hulls laden with heroin and marijuana and sped unfettered over the 90 miles across the Gulf Stream to Key West. The web of organization included the timing of trucks at the docks to haul the illicit drugs to Miami under the auspices of Trafficante mobsters and drug dealers.

Despite Key West's diminutive dimensions of 1.25 miles at its widest point and four miles long, its population still represented the largest concentration of residents and businesses scattered throughout the chain of islands that make up the Florida Keys. In a crowded little town like Key West, rumors became facts and facts became rumors, particularly as they pertained to Mafia presence. FBI files on Key West Mafia ties and activities were opened in the 1950s and swelled through the 1960s. That was when names started turning up in those reports like Farto, Trafficante, Teamsters Union President Jimmy Hoffa and Teamsters operatives Sam "The Fat Man" Cagnina and Raimundo Beiro.

As in all small communities, a web of connections existed. Allegedly, Cagnina was a nephew of Santo Trafficante, and besides doing the bidding of the Teamsters Union he ran a crew in Key West involved in all aspects of organized crime. One law enforcement source listed Cagnina and his accomplice Beiro as cousins. Bum Farto, a lifelong Conch—the moniker bestowed on native Key Westers—could not have been ignorant of all these happenings and familial relationships, particularly considering that in 1955 he'd married Beiro's sister, Estelle.

Even in the southernmost city of the Lower 48 states, deep dark secrets could not be hidden from the rest of the world forever, and Florida's Governor LeRoy Collins would soon take action. But before that hammer fell, other events shook the island and the world. First, Batista fled Cuba on January 1, 1959, before Castro could arrest him. Since the inevitable defeat of Batista's troops could be foretold months previously, he flew out of Havana to Portugal, likely with enough cash to last four or five lifetimes (he died in 1973).

Castro immediately shut down the Mafia operations and nationalized everything in the mold of the Soviet Union, which had been secretly funding and abetting his revolution. Not surprisingly and yet to Eisenhower's horror, Castro publicly declared his allegiance to communism. The start of the Castro dictatorship also meant that the Havana to Key West to Miami drug artery no longer flowed.

The Mafia was none too happy to lose such a perfect setup. Nevertheless, things went on as usual in Key West with shipments of narcotics coming from ports other than Havana to the city and other drop points up the line of islands. But the mob's troubles in Key West took another hit on January 1, 1961. Governor Collins made his move—the "Bubba Bust," consisting of 40 arrests. That included local bolita kingpin Louis "Blackie" Fernandez along with his coterie of ticket sellers and accomplices; undercover cops packed up and left for home.

Undaunted, once the dust had cleared Trafficante restarted bolita operations and took control of the island's police and fire departments. The Tampa Mafia did the same with Key West's commission and the trucking and construction unions—the latter orchestrated by frequent Key West visitor Jimmy Hoffa. By controlling shipments of goods to Key West via U.S. 1—the only road connecting Key West with Florida's mainland—the mob could extort local businesses. Teamsters' money flowed into ownership of Key West resorts, a shopping center, and, as a PR gesture, a seven-figure check was donated to the local hospital.

Bum Farto weathered the storms. In 1964 as the new fire chief, he set out to prove he wasn't merely going to keep the seat warm. With fervor and bravado, he upgraded the fire department's trucks and gear, boosted the staff's morale, provided free safety inspections, quickened notifications when a fire was reported, and improved fire truck response time. To feed his ego, Farto proudly referred to himself as "El Jefe," Spanish for The Chief. Over the next 12 years he helped rescue Cuban refugees and provided them safety and comfort—hey, not even bad people are all bad. But one thing Farto didn't know: He and his fire department were on the feds' radar screen. One such investigation—Operation Conch—would prove to be his Waterloo.

On September 9, 1975, state and federal law enforcement authorities made their move, resulting in Farto's arrest. He'd been caught red-handed selling drugs to an undercover agent. Besides Farto, the city attorney and 27 others went down as well—mostly those with Miami drug ties. As further details emerged, Farto was accused of using the fire station as a base of operations to sell cocaine. The news created shock waves throughout Key West and resurrected persistent rumors about Farto's coziness with organized crime figures. His reputation and many good works spiraled down the drain.

As quickly as the ink dried on Farto's arrest warrant, whispers centered on who else he and the others might take down with them. Sentenced to 30 years, Farto damn sure knew the fate of potential squealers facing long prison terms. The news about Operation Conch immediately spread, reaching the ears of Santo Trafficante, New York Mafiosi, and drug kingpins in Miami and Colombia. Facing either decades of decay in a cell or his corpse being eaten by sharks, on February 16, 1976, Farto put his taillights to Key West and likely drove exactly at the speed limit to Miami—his car was discovered there two months later. He'd jumped bail, a real Farto vanishing in the wind.

Did he go on the lam to another country? No records suggested such. Did he get silenced by the Mafia or drug lords? No proof of that exists. In fact, his body—like that of Jimmy Hoffa, who coincidentally disappeared five weeks prior to Farto's arrest—has never been found. An all-points bulletin and periodic manhunts proved fruitless. The years peeled off the calender. Anyone who knew anything about the whereabouts or getaway plans or death of Bum Farto kept mum. Finally, he was declared dead.

Whether he passed away long ago (he'd now be over 100) or made it to a safe haven is anyone's guess. But I'll state my theory. It's likely that Farto was the driver of his car to Miami, where drug contacts lived. The fact that he jumped bail signaled his intent never to cooperate with law enforcement, which the Mafia realized. But at the same time, they knew if he got caught he could still do a plea deal. In other words, Farto reckoned that he needed to escape to a place offering a decent lifestyle with a new identity where no one could finger him. The Bahamian and Caribbean islands were too small to remain incognito. He wouldn't go to Cuba because while he may have been chummy with Castro during his visits to Key West over a decade earlier, Farto realized that the new Cuban dictator wouldn't be keen harboring an American drug fugitive. In fact, Castro might even use Farto as trade bait with the U.S.

Ergo, I believe that a former drug contact in Miami helped Farto obtain forged ID and concealed him for a few weeks. Farto then hopped aboard a private plane or boat and hightailed it across the Gulf of Mexico. I conclude that Farto ended up in Costa Rica for two reasons: It's one of the more pleasant and stable countries in Central America, and in 1976 living outside the capital city of San Jose pretty much assured anonymity.

Guesswork aside, Joseph "Bum" Farto's disappearance remains a mystery over 50 years later. But the evolving lure of drug money in the Florida Keys hardly ceased. In fact, it escalated, and if the players weren't quite as colorful in name or action as Farto, the fever from suitcases stuffed with Ben Franklins infected the hearts of many notable Keys figures.

The growing popularity of the Keys as a fishing and diving mecca resulted in ever-increasing boat traffic, particularly during the 1970s and '80s. That made it difficult for the Drug Enforcement Administration (DEA), FBI, Coast Guard and other agencies to discern whether charter captains were fishing clients in the Gulf Stream or aiding in the smuggling of drugs. Besides the lure of money, some of the very people charged with enforcement of laws controlling drug use and sales were themselves users. In 1980, the *Miami Herald* reported that Monroe County State Attorney Jeff Gautier exhibited a fondness for weed and other substances, after which Governor Bob Graham removed him from office.

I knew the *Herald* report to be true. My father-in-law at the time, Capt. Grady Patrick, often fished with Gautier in the late 1970s and they became tight friends. My then wife and I were invited to a party at the two-story Key Largo home of Phil Knight, a Miami trial judge, who some believed was soft on marijuana cases that came before him. Although Knight was not there that night, Gautier sat on the couch with a large paper bag stuffed with marijuana, rolling joints no amateur could fashion. He even hit on my wife, after which he apologized when realizing she was Capt. Patrick's daughter. Wow, and this was the guy prosecuting drug offenders in Monroe County?

The hustles went on and on. In 1984 the entire Key West Police Department was deemed "a criminal enterprise" by the FBI after a two-year sting operation. Deputy Police Chief Raymond "Tito" Casamayor Jr., along with two of his detectives, got nailed and convicted of protecting drug smugglers. The investigation also exposed a $16 million cocaine business operated out of Key West's city hall—shades of Bum Farto and his fire department! Further amusement: One of the dealers used Burger King bags to deliver drugs to Casamayor, and they didn't include the kind of Coke that refreshes.

In the 1980s several members of the Coast Guard stationed at the base in Islamorada on Snake Creek got arrested, including the son of one of my friends. The Coasties tipped off druggies as to where and when law enforcement vessels would be present. I never did find out how much money they took in exchange for the inside information, but it resulted in dishonorable discharges and criminal plea deals.

When I was living in Tavernier near the north end of the Keys in the late 1980s and early 1990s, the home of a law enforcement officer—I think he worked for the Marine Patrol—got raided based on an anonymous tip. It led to the discovery of an unexplained $50,000 in cash stashed in the freezer of the officer's refrigerator. Cold cash indeed.

In 1995 Emery Major, a Key West commissioner, pled guilty to bribery and extortion charges. In 2005 Monroe County Mayor Jack London died just before being sentenced for tax evasion. In 2007 Monroe County State's Attorney Jim Hendrick received a guilty verdict for witness tampering, conspiracy, and obstruction of justice. In 2013 a Florida Keys deputy sheriff was caught buying fake oxycodone pills while in a marked police car.

Even today, Keys boaters or beach goers sometimes encounter a "square grouper"—a bale of marijuana wrapped in plastic—floating in the Gulf Stream or washed ashore. They somehow occasionally escape from a cache meant to be scooped up by a boat or freighter in the Gulf Stream, which lies just a few miles from the Keys in the Atlantic Ocean. I discovered just such a bale near the shoreline of Key Largo one day while boating with my family and dutifully called the Coast Guard on channel 16 of my VHF radio.

Two dour officers showed up in a boat nearly an hour later, tied up to mine, and proceeded to spend over an hour grilling me, my wife, and two small children. They then inspected every inch of my boat and one dived into the water with a mask to view the hull. They left with the bale and not even a thank you. So much for being a good citizen; it became obvious that they were purposely discouraging me from bothering them again with such a trivial matter. No wonder good citizens often turned bad or looked the other way.

Jorge Cabrera became one of the more notorious drug dealers in the Keys from the late 1980s through the mid-1990s. According to former Islamorada charter captains I knew, Cabrera would bribe coastal residents in the Upper Keys zone now known as Millionaires Row, which features large private homes. He offered the homeowners $100,000 cash to disappear for a week on vacation somewhere; it was an offer no one refused. Cabrera's crew would then use the home's dockage to receive huge shipments of marijuana and cocaine. By switching reception points, Cabrera avoided detection for years.

Cabrera and other drug dealers often utilized charter boat captains fishing out of various marinas in Key Largo and Islamorada to do the drop-offs. Law enforcement became habituated to local boats coming in and out of ports all day and at first seldom boarded them, especially when it appeared they carried divers or anglers. The aforementioned Capt. Grady Patrick confided that he regularly turned down offers from drug smugglers, sometimes for as much as $10,000, to make an occasional single drug pickup in the Gulf Stream—where a ship or airplane would dump the wrapped and floating cargo into the water—and take it to Key Largo. He'd be given the drop-off and pickup locations if cooperating. I know Patrick turned it down because he was almost always broke.

Others, however, did not turn the offers down. The late veteran Islamorada skipper Don Gurgiolo chartered out of what was then Holiday Isle Resort & Marina, for which I worked as director of resort and marina operations in the early 1990s. I got to know Don and really liked him, and no skipper could spot fish better. He got busted in a drug takedown and went to prison, after which he returned to the Keys and set up a ministry of sorts to dissuade others from making the mistake he did.

Cabrera faced a dilemma often involved with the constant influx of mass quantities of unreported cash—how to wash it inconspicuously. He decided to invest in real estate in Atlantic City and the Keys. He also became a big shot in the Democrat Party and met Hillary Clinton, Al Gore, and other bigwigs. He contributed $20,000 to the Democratic National Committee earmarked for Bill Clinton's 1996 reelection campaign. When Cabrera got sentenced to 19 years in prison in October 1996 for drug smuggling, the DNC quickly returned the check. According to Cabrera in news reports—he didn't respond to my requests for an interview—the government confiscated all of Cabrera's money, cars, trucks, boats and airplanes. After serving 15 years of his sentence, Cabrera returned to Islamorada, expressed regret for his past drug involvement, and lived with his wife Angel and engaged in lawful businesses until his death in August 2022.

Of course, Cabrera was hardly the only guy offering the use of others' property to engage in illegal activities. Treasure hunter Carl "Fizz" Fismer, a friend with residences in the Keys and Tampa, tells this story about a man and his wife without naming names even though he said they're deceased: "A friend of mine and his wife used to manage a small motel in Islamorada. About every other month a man would rent all rooms for one night for $10,000—cash, of course. They'd ask no questions, go to Miami, get a room, enjoy dinner and a movie, and return the next afternoon."

Don't let all that scare you from visiting the Keys. I know of no negative incidents involving tourists. If you enjoy the island lifestyle, like to fish or dive or just soak in the subtropical sun with a rum runner or margarita, you'll love it there. It's a nice getaway and I still visit often.

4

A MOB MURDER?

Have you ever heard of Puzuzu, the mythical flying demon that brings famines and bad luck to anyone brushed by its wings? Probably not, and the same applied to Konstantinos "Gus" Boulis, a Greek immigrant whose meteoric rise as an entrepreneur in South Florida ended when he brushed wings with the wrong people. As history has recorded over and over again, it's one thing to cavort with those connected to Puzuzu—my euphemism for the Mafia—but if you do so it can be fatal.

You have heard the saying about quitting when you're ahead. Undoubtedly so did Boulis, but it didn't sink in. How did he amass millions of dollars and end up murdered at age 51? It almost certainly stemmed from an ill-fated decision to get into the casino business.

After being born and raised in Greece, Gus Boulis eschewed becoming a fisherman like his father. In 1971 at age 22, he took a 16-year-old bride to avoid a Greek deportation issue, had two sons with her, and left them behind four years later by going AWOL when stepping off a merchant marine ship in Canada. Boulis found employment in a Mr. Submarine store in Toronto and soon talked the owners into franchising, and they followed his lead and made him a partner. In five years the business boomed to nearly 200 stores.

After selling his interest, Boulis moved to the Florida Keys in 1977. But instead of kicking back as a youthful multimillionaire and enjoying the sunshine and his penchant for ladies, his workaholic drive swamped any ideas about a leisurely existence. He got back into the restaurant business and again built an empire. Along the way Boulis met 18-year-old Margaret Hren and took her under his wing. Literally. For the next 16 years, she became his assistant and girlfriend with whom he had two more sons. He started a seafood restaurant in Key Largo called The Quay—an instant hit with locals and tourists—and a sub store on Duval Street in Key West.

Meanwhile, Boulis had turned his knowledge in the sub business into another booming chain beginning in 1989 called Miami Subs, with franchises throughout Florida. One such location turned out to be Joe Sonken's Gold Coast Restaurant and Lounge in Hollywood, Florida—a reputed mob hangout at the time.

He next obtained financing as a developer for a huge project, the Marriott Key Largo Resort. Boulis also bought a hotel in Hollywood, Florida, and soon owned a Lear jet and a yacht. Everything Boulis touched turned to gold, and he became renowned in South Florida for his generosity and support to the Greek community.

During the span from the late 1980s into the mid-'90s I lived in Tavernier, a flyspeck of a town in the Upper Keys. I met Gus Boulis in 1985 after he'd moved to Hollywood, Florida, because he was often in the Keys pursuing his burgeoning business interests. Boulis wanted to include a watersports operator at his Marriott resort and engaged in subcontracting negotiations with my friend in Key Largo, Darrell McCullough. McCullough and wife Jean already ran a successful business in the Keys, offering personal watercraft, sailboats, parasailing and the like. Through the McCulloughs I met Boulis and immediately found him to be gregarious, friendly and unpretentious. Despite his money and jet-set lifestyle, he wore shorts and Polo shirts that seemed to enhance his blondish hair and blue eyes, all carried with a confidence that attracted many women.

Boulis knew how to draw people in with his charisma, money and easy-going demeanor—the latter of which concealed a terrible temper that would later get him into beaucoup hot water. In our chats, he reminisced about helping his dad in the fishing business in Greece during his boyhood, knowing that this chimed with my side interest as a freelance writer for travel and fishing magazines. At one point I mused that it would be cool to have my own publication.

"I'll partner with you," he said quickly, pouncing on the opening. "I'll put up the capital, you organize a staff and the content and work up a viable business plan, and we'll make it the most successful fishing-travel magazine in the world."

Sounded good to me, and I got busy putting together a business plan. But it never got off the ground because that was about the time Boulis made a critical mistake. Evidently his success as an entrepreneur involved a bit of gambler's blood, so he figured he'd also roll a 7 and become a mogul in the casino business. And for a few years, he was right.

Boulis's fondness for gambling apparently grew out of a 1994 event when he leased an entire ship to take several hundred Miami Subs employees on a day trip off Key Largo. When the skipper announced they were in

Konstantinos "Gus" Boulis became a successful restaurateur before making the tragic mistake of becoming involved in the casino business with alleged Mafia figures. The SunCruz Casino line offered gambling cruises. (© *Tampa Bay Times*/ZUMA Press)

international waters after only cruising three miles offshore, Boulis's mind whirled like a slot machine. He most certainly knew that in international waters, he and everyone aboard the ship could do just about anything they wanted. To hell with selling $5 subs one at a time; he could make 50 times that on each roll on a craps table.

That employee trip set in motion instant action. Boulis stepped down as the day-to-day president of Miami Subs, keeping just a financial interest until he sold the 192-store chain in 1999 to the Nathan's Famous food chain. Boulis bought a small ship and outfitted it with slot machines, a craps table, blackjack tables, a full liquor bar and a bevy of handpicked cute waitresses. The operation immediately proved to be popular, with the ship going out fully booked on every trip.

Encouraged by the massive influx of green money and no oversight by bureaucrats, that same year Boulis launched SunCruz Casinos. No longer did Floridians and tourists who fancied gambling have to go to the Bahamas or wing it to Las Vegas or Atlantic City. Instead, they could drive to Key Largo and, in less than an hour, be sitting in front of a one-armed bandit or playing blackjack, and all this in the Gulf Stream beyond the reach of U.S. laws.

Boulis soon acquired 10 more gambling ships in Florida and another in South Carolina. The ships kept getting larger—the *SunCruz VI* berthed in Hollywood carried up to 600 passengers. The cash poured in from Sun-Cruz to Boulis, and his bank account swelled even further with the sale of Miami Subs for $14 million. Flush with cash and able to guarantee hefty bank notes, Boulis became an investor in several swank South Florida resort hotel projects.

While his business interests flourished, all hell broke loose at once in his personal life. In October 1997 Margaret Hren, now his former girlfriend but still mother of two of his four sons, had Boulis arrested for harassment and physical abuse. She also obtained a restraining order against him as they battled for custody of their children. Months later Efrosini "Frances" Boulis, his wife in Greece—they had separated in 1976 but hadn't divorced—and mother of his original two sons, filed for divorce in early 1998 and laid claim for half his assets. Boulis hired a probate attorney in 1999 and drew up a will that was upheld in court, listing the two sons by Hren as heirs but for whatever reason excluding his Greek family.

His troubles, however, were far from over and about to get even worse. In 1998 a nine-month investigation by Florida's attorney general and the sheriff of Broward County revealed that Boulis's gambling ships often didn't go beyond three miles from shore. They seized three of his ships and confiscated gambling equipment and $630,000 in cash. Boulis went to court against that seizure and won on a technicality.

But the government wouldn't relent. Licensing research revealed that Boulis had bought the initial six gambling ships in 1994 in the name of then girlfriend Margaret Hren because Boulis wasn't a U.S. citizen at the time, a requirement for ownership. In a sealed document by the U.S. attorney, charges regarding that issue were dropped, but Boulis received a fine of $500,000 personally and his companies were fined another $500,000. On top of that, he was ordered to sell all of his interest in SunCruz within three years. Little did the government or Boulis foresee that this order would cost him his life.

In September 2000 Boulis sold SunCruz for $147.5 million, but he did not exercise very good due diligence in selecting the new owners. The buyers turned out to be former Washington lobbyist Jack Abramoff and Dial-A-Mattress founder Adam Kidan. The deal included a $20 million promissory note instead of a previously agreed upon down payment of $23 million—the latter supposedly to be kept in a trust account. But secret handshake deals also transpired, and that along with the questionable trust account would later prove to be a legal albatross for Abramoff and Kidan.

In a dubious move suggesting that Boulis didn't think the government would ever find out about it, he worked out an arrangement with the new owners to keep him in the deal with 10 percent of net revenue plus to be put on the books as a "consultant" for $250,000 per year. Boulis signed a non-compete agreement stating he wouldn't get involved in the gambling ship business. By this time, SunCruz had swelled to 1,150 employees with prodigious eight-digit annual profits. The ships in Florida were ported in Key Largo, Hollywood, Fort Myers, Tampa, Port Canaveral and Daytona Beach. As this was a mainly offshore cash business, it's anyone's guess if revenue received equaled revenue reported.

This is when the story gets *really* ugly. The relationship with Abramoff and Kidan went sour almost immediately. First was the questionable character of Abramoff, who would later be a convicted felon and serve nearly four years in prison after pleading guilty to mail fraud, tax evasion, and conspiracy to bribe public officials. Boulis accused Kidan, the new chairman of SunCruz, of stealing $3 million in cash from the ships and forcing him along with some of his trusted employees and family members out of the business. Kidan in turn accused Boulis of stealing slot machines to set up a cruise-to-nowhere operation of his own, leading to mutual lawsuits. On top of that, five lawsuits were filed against SunCruz by an assortment of investors and managers who felt they were getting swindled.

The straw that broke the camel's back came during a heated argument in Kidan's office when—according to Kidan—Boulis went into a manic rage, threatening to kill him and even lunging at him with a pen. Kidan obtained a restraining order and hired a security company to dig into Boulis's past, resulting in a report citing violent tendencies.

You can draw your own conclusions as to what happened next. Kiran hired as a consultant Anthony "Big Tony" Moscatiello—a reputed Gambino crime family member and an associate of John Gotti—and Anthony "Little Tony" Ferrari as a security consultant, also allegedly with Gambino ties.

On February 6, 2001, after a series of business meetings at his office building at 910 S.E. 17th St. in Fort Lauderdale, Boulis left just after 9 p.m. in his BMW. A few blocks away, a car cut him off and forced a stop. Seconds later a black Mustang arrived on the scene and the driver rapid-fired a handgun, with three of the bullets ripping into Boulis's body. The two cars screeched away and the bloodied Boulis managed to drive off, but a block away he crashed into a tree. After being rushed to Broward General Medical Hospital, Boulis died hours later from the bullet wounds.

So who murdered Boulis? Maybe Adam Kidan or even the shady Jack Abramoff? Abramoff's unsavory reputation involved political misdoings but not acts of violence. Boulis had threatened to kill Kidan, and perhaps this was a way for Kidan to strike first, especially because Boulis was also demanding $30 million from him in unpaid SunCruz profits. But it's unlikely that a white-collar guy like Kidan would have been the trigger man—especially since Kidan was in Europe when Boulis was ambushed.

This murder smacked of a gangland-style professional hit. That brought into the lineup of suspects Kidan's SunCruz hires of Moscatiello and Ferrari. Speculation was that both men likely felt a need to protect their lucrative income in SunCruz by disposing of the ever-meddling Gus Boulis. But the police couldn't figure it all out, and the case went cold for over a decade.

While Abramoff and Kidan dodged any rap for Boulis's murder, the government bagged them on another corner. It involved the questionable down payment deal with Boulis in the sale of SunCruz. On August 11, 2005, Abramoff and Kidan took guilty pleas for committing fraud and received long sentences that were shortened when they cooperated with government prosecutors. A month later, investigators finally arrested three men for the 2001 execution-style murder of Boulis: Moscatiello, Ferrari, and a third accused conspirator, James "Pudgy" Fiorillo.

After numerous court delays fashioned by attorneys for the defendants, first-degree murder charges were filed in Broward County against Moscatiello and Ferrari along with conspiracy to commit murder and solicitation to commit murder. Fiorillo was also charged with first-degree murder and conspiracy to commit murder. Fiorillo pled guilty and testified for the prosecution, receiving a six-year sentence. Finally in 2015, in separate trials, Ferrari was convicted of first-degree murder and Moscatiello was found guilty of first-degree murder and conspiracy to commit murder. Both received life sentences without parole.

Those convictions did not end the controversy. The water became even murkier about who killed Gus Boulis in May 2006 when Adam Kidan stated that Moscatiello and Ferrari had told him privately that John Gurino, a John Gotti associate, was the gunman in the Mustang. That finger-pointing may have been true, but in any event that seemed quite convenient because Gurino—who hadn't been a suspect—could no longer dispute the accusation, having been killed in October 2003 during an altercation with the owner of a delicatessen. With only hearsay evidence and no proof or confession, Gurino escaped blame. And even if it was true, Gurino obviously did not act alone.

But that is still not the end of the Gus Boulis story. In 2018 new trials for Moscatiello and Ferrari were reordered on appeal, and the following year the Florida Supreme Court agreed. The ruling concurred that the juries in each trial should not have been told by a witness that the actual killer was John Gurino and that Moscatiello orchestrated it.

Moscatiello, approaching his 80s, and Ferrari, in his mid-60s, have always maintained their innocence. However, in January 2022, Moscatiello and Ferrari accepted a plea deal to second-degree murder, with 10- and 18-year sentences respectively.

It seems that anything to do with fast boats and casinos draws the attention of mobsters. Something similar to Boulis's demise took place years earlier with Miami's Don Aronow, one of the pioneers of offshore racing. Aronow, the maker of fast racing boats that enabled smugglers to avoid or outrun Coast Guard vessels, was assassinated in 1987 in gangland style outside his northeast Miami office by a cocaine trafficker named Bobby Young. Prosecutors asserted that Young was hired by marijuana smuggler Benjamin Kramer to do the hit because of Kramer's business dispute with Aronow. Kramer became somewhat famous for attempting to escape prison in 1990 in a helicopter. The attempt failed when the chopper crashed.

But back to Boulis. It's been quite a challenge to piece together the complicated life of Gus Boulis. Like that of Bum Farto in chapter 3, Boulis's life still remains controversial. Too much ambition combined with greed guided him to the wings of Puzuzu, otherwise he'd still likely be around today.

5

SCARFACE SEGUES TO MIAMI

Soon after the Gay 90s and turn of the century in Florida, scattered villages became towns and towns became cities. Small pockets of organized crime sprang up in varying levels, with the typical progression from small-time street gangs to the notorious rise of the Ku Klux Klan. But what really put the Sunshine State into the consciousness of America's burgeoning underworld was none other than Alphonse Gabriel "Scarface" Capone.

As boss for seven years during Prohibition of The Outfit—an organized crime syndicate that controlled Chicago politics and illegal activities—Capone enjoyed national marquee status. Newsreels often showed the burly mobster chomping stogies and sporting fedoras as he swaggered in and out of limos accompanied by even burlier bodyguards. By wresting control of the Windy City's bootlegging, speakeasies, gambling and prostitution operations, he multiplied his net worth to over $100 million.

Preceding him as Chicago's boss was Vincenzo Colosimo, a.k.a. "Diamond Jim" and "Big Jim." Colosimo was murdered on May 11, 1920, and Johnny Torrio took over with Capone as top gun in his mob—in fact, they were boyhood friends and partners in crime at an early age. Five years later, however, in 1925, Torrio barely survived his own murder and decided to call it quits. At the age of 26 Scarface took charge of The Outfit.

A few years after Prohibition began in 1920 and before Torrio left the scene, Capone ventured to Key West and Cuba with Torrio to set up another distribution source for booze other than Canada and New York. Capone also bought land parcels in St. Petersburg in 1925 during the Florida land boom with Torrio and two others in his name and under a corporation named Manro. By the late 1920s—particularly 1927, when Chicago's mayor and police chief turned up the heat on him—Capone started thinking about a quieter life away from the Windy City, even if part-time. Somewhere warm, perhaps. He checked out cities in California but found himself unwelcome.

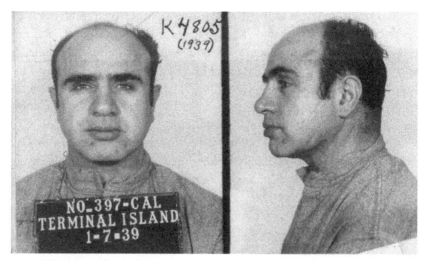

K 4805
(1939)

NO. 397-CAL
TERMINAL ISLAND
1-7-39

Famed Chicago mobster Alphonse "Scarface" Capone's mug shots in 1939. (Federal Bureau of Investigation)

In looking for a retirement locale, Capone passed up his St. Petersburg properties because some of them had tax liens filed by the IRS and were seized after his tax evasion conviction. He knew Miami to be a bustling town and more to his liking, plus at least initially he encountered a friendly reception. He'd already visited the Magic City many times over the years when taking flights to and from Cuba. Using fake names, Capone leased a home in Miami Beach's exclusive Indian Creek neighborhood and a penthouse suite at the Ponce de Leon Hotel in downtown Miami. He and wife Mae and son Sonny became entranced by the tropical breezes and the sweep of coconut palms dotting the waterfront. His vision of a more relaxed setting for his family became a nice lifestyle change from the hectic, violent scene in Chicago.

Even for someone who enjoyed media attention, a respite from the pressured kill-or-be-killed existence in Chicago must have been appealing. In 1928 Capone was shown a home on Palm Island, a ritzy man-made spit of land just east of the southern portion of Miami Beach in Biscayne Bay. It had a nice security feature: The island could only be accessed via one small bridge or by boat. Residents consisted exclusively of a wealthy set who could afford waterfront estates—it was not a place for the riffraff or the rowdy. Capone agreed to pay $30,000 for a 100 by 300-foot property at 93 Palm Avenue on the east side of the island.

There existed on the property a two-story, Spanish-tiled residence with seven bedrooms. That wouldn't be sufficient for Capone's family and entourage, however. He set about overseeing improvements that included a surrounding seven-foot concrete wall fronted by an iron gate, a two-story lodge to accommodate his bodyguards and guests, fountains and gardens, a huge swimming pool separating the lodge from the waterfront residence, and a T-shaped dock with a small boathouse.

All the construction and commotion didn't go unnoticed by Palm Islanders. Displeased by the raucous late-night noise and occasional gunshots from partiers at the Capone compound, the homeowners' association attempted to dislodge him, but to no avail. A deed existed on the property that eventually ended up in Mae's name, and unless a serious crime took place, nothing could be done to sack the infamous Scarface and his entourage from the island.

The Chamber of Commerce voiced concern, as did the Women's Club. Miami Beach's Mayor Lummus—also a realtor, who initially showed the Palm Island property to Capone—and the city manager met with the gangster and came away claiming to all that Capone only sought peaceful solitude. Even Florida Governor Doyle Carlton was horrified when the news reached him in Tallahassee of Capone's new winter residence. Without any legal justification, Carlton rashly implored the state's lawmen to go out and arrest the Chicagoan. That went nowhere, and a judge issued an injunction to stop harassing Capone. Besides staying a step ahead of Floridians who'd never coped with a major league mobster, he sweet-talked the Miami police chief and key local business and political leaders, convincing them that he meant no harm and in fact would enrich the local and state economy.

Just to prove he wasn't merely a silver-tongued devil, Capone wasted no time writing big checks to local charities and to the coffers of office holders and candidates. Waiters and doormen around town received $100 tips. Yes indeed, one of America's most infamous mobsters had hopefully turned over a new leaf, leaving behind allegations of murders and mayhem to become a good Samaritan.

Sending another message, Capone made it known that he'd retained top-shelf attorneys to discourage legal squabbles, and as things turned out they were kept busy. Suspicion arose that through a third party, Scarface had attempted to buy the *Miami Daily News* so that he could control the media narrative and stop the paper's incessant criticism of him, but that failed when publisher James Cox wouldn't sell—not even for the overpriced offer of half a million dollars.

Capone's home on Palm Island near Miami Beach became a scene of noisy gatherings, much to the chagrin of his neighbors and then Governor Doyle Carlton. (floridamemory.com)

Given his nefarious reputation, those not on the receiving end of Capone's generosity fought his presence in Miami, and they doubted that Capone would retire with a life of philanthropy and fishing. Of course, they were right. Zebras don't change their stripes, and while the Chicagoan may have unfurled the Sunshine State's welcome mat for other soon-to-come big-name mobsters, he already knew about the existing scale of illegal gambling activities that preceded him by decades. All forms of games of chance flourished in South Florida, including fancy resort casinos dotting Florida's east coast owned by railroad magnate Henry Flagler.

Capone and major organized crime figures also learned that way back in 1913—well before the federal National Prohibition Act went into effect—Dade County had passed a referendum restricting alcohol use. Miami banned bars in residential areas and cut the operating hours of bars elsewhere. Almost instantly, rum boats raced from Bimini in the Bahamas to the outskirts of Miami, where cases of booze were transferred to myriad smaller boats, making it impossible for the Coast Guard to stop, inspect, and arrest all but a handful.

Even today it seems that the last consideration of lawmakers is whether enforceability of what they're passing is practical. It's meaningless to restrict activities for all when well-organized people with bad intentions can always get away with it. The sad lesson of Prohibition and acts to deny what the public wants revealed that Uncle Sam can pass moralistic laws until the cows come home, but banning won't work. Drinking alcohol, prostitution, and illegal gambling will still go on behind the scenes without the nuisance of obtaining licenses and paying taxes. Adding to the allure of setting up illegal operations: Florida's legal system prior to the 1950s, being naïve about corruption and what convictions did occur, netted sentences too paltry to inhibit sagacious Mafiosi like Capone.

Pre-dating the arrival of Capone was also the fact that no city roared more in the Roaring 20s than Miami, what with horse racing parlors and swanky clubs crammed with high rollers. And nobody seemed overly concerned as bolita games proliferated. Even when periodic raids occurred as a media PR show, usually the gambling establishments had been tipped off and no ringleaders were apprehended.

The nature of Al Capone being what it was, he wanted more than a share of the Florida action; he wanted to control it. He envisioned building another Chicago fiefdom without the gangland infighting and with his brothers, cousins, and henchman controlling gambling as the financial headliner and branching out to whatever other crimes made for easy pickings.

No sooner had he sought to calm fears about whether he'd be a good boy, than Capone set up a bootlegging route from the Bahamas to Deerfield Beach, under the guise of a commercial fishing venture. Everyone in Florida loved to dine on fish, and Capone's boats went out at night with false bottoms to stash cases of liquor in the hulls. And just to make trips to Deerfield Beach more cost effective, Capone opened a speakeasy in the area.

When on February 14, 1929, the crime played out in Chicago that will be forever known as the St. Valentine's Day Massacre, Capone visited the Dade County Courthouse to discuss allegations of his involvement with the murder of former rival Frankie Yale in New York. At the same time on the north side of Chicago, likely at least two of his hit men costumed as cops herded seven members of rival mobster Bugs Moran's gang into a warehouse and proceeded to aerate them with tommy gun slugs. Though strongly suspected of involvement with both the Chicago and New York killings, Scarface never was charged for them. Instead, he received a contempt charge for not showing up to testify before a grand jury. He served less than a year in a Pennsylvania prison cell that was more like a hotel room, allowing him to handle Outfit business without interruption. Everyone scoffed at Capone's Miami alibi, but no one who may have been involved and wanted to protect his or her personal safety squealed.

In April 1930 Capone along with family members and bodyguards returned to Miami amid a renewed outcry to banish him from the state.

While he fended off all such attempts—enduring constant arrests and ha-rassment for violations as trivial as vagrancy—it soon became apparent that retirement was not going to be hassle free, and law enforcement saw through any pretense of Capone being just another snowbird in Miami. In addition to his Deerfield Beach operations, Capone bought into the Florid-ian Hotel and other gambling establishments as well as the South Beach dog track. Allegations of rigged games and skimming arose, and he even tried but failed to control the bookmaking rackets, losing out to the power-ful S&G syndicate.

What eventually led to Al Capone's downfall involved him contracting syphilis from a Chicago prostitute, the IRS nailing him for tax evasion, and violations of the National Prohibition Act. Convicted and sent to an Atlanta prison in May 1932 and later to Alcatraz in San Francisco, the once mighty mobster found his physical and mental health deteriorating. He was released in November 1939 so that he could receive treatment at Johns Hopkins Hospital in Baltimore and infirmaries in California and Pennsyl-vania for late-stage syphilis. He returned to Miami a broken man. He died from a stroke a week after his birthday at age 48 at his beloved home on Palm Island. Mae sold the property in 1952 and died in 1996 in Hollywood, Florida, still professing her love for Alphonse Gabriel Capone.

But Capone's bold move to Florida in 1928 signaled other cold-weather mobsters to follow in his footsteps. The roots of the Mafia were already established in Tampa, and those connections with the five crime families in New York City and beyond opened a floodgate. With Capone in prison and Prohibition ending in 1933 to put an end to bootlegging, gambling took the lead as organized crime's profit incentive. And that would prove to be law enforcement's biggest headache, especially as it mushroomed in South Florida and neighboring Cuba in the 1940s and '50s. The small-time bolita dealers operating out of private homes, dingy bars, and from nighttime street corners in the Latin sectors didn't pose much of a threat to society. *La Cosa Nostra,* on the other hand, posed a massive threat.

Via millions in washed money and life-threatening intimidation, the Mafia could buy and control everything from small newsstands to major hotels and beach resorts. The revenue streams swelled as rich northerners arrived for the sunshine and to play the tables, cavort in expensive suites, guzzle top-shelf booze and hire high-priced ladies. And let's say you can't cover your markers, pal? No problem, just pay it back with shylocking in-terest rates or you might end up on crutches or with compromising pic-tures sent to your wife.

Upcoming chapters dig into the activities of some of the Mafiosi who followed Capone's Florida migration in the 1930s through the early 1960s, such as Meyer Lansky, Vincent Alo, Pasquale Erra, and hundreds of others. While Kefauver's hearings made it clear that the Mafia existed and controlled numerous gambling establishments in Florida and elsewhere, the Mafia did not abandon the state—particularly in Tampa. Drug lords also loomed in the crosshairs of law enforcement and still do so to this day. Following are their stories and those of some of the incorruptible characters who tried to stop them.

6

LANSKY & FLORIDA GAMBLING

Although Al Capone's part-time residency in Miami in 1928 caused quite a stir, a man who would change the landscape of the criminal world far more dramatically arrived in South Florida a year later. In contrast to Scarface, he eschewed showmanship and publicity. But like Capone's Palm Island residence, he also bought a Spanish-style home, and his presence became a more powerful magnet for the arrival of numerous wise guys from all corners of the nation.

Records of his birth name vary: Meier Suchowlanski, Meyer Suchowlansky, and Majer Suchowlijas. He is better known simply as Meyer Lansky. He was born in early July 1902—the precise day is uncertain—in Grodno, Russia (now Belarus). Meyer's father Max arrived at Ellis Island in 1909 and sent for wife Yetta and Meyer in 1911. The Jewish immigrants first moved in with Max's parents in the Lower East Side of New York City.

In not being Italian or a seasoned street fighter, Meyer found the tough guys didn't pay him much attention even as he became a teenager. Although he stood only 5'5" tall—even in elevated shoes—the nickname of "Little Man" by his soon-to-be mob peers recognized the irony that he was far from little when it came to wielding power at the highest levels of the Mafia.

Even as a scrawny kid, Lansky would fight back like a cornered rat if assaulted. He had become pals with neighborhood tough Benjamin "Bugsy" Siegel, who stuck up for Lansky and later formed with him the "Bugs & Meyer Mob." When street thug Charles "Lucky" Luciano tried to extort him one day in 1920, the 18-year-old Lansky would have none of it.

Luciano admired the little guy's pluckiness, and the two teamed up with Siegel as friends and partners in crime. As fate would have it, nearly three decades later in 1947, allegedly, Lansky would reluctantly agree to a mob hit put on Siegel for mismanagement and missing funds at the Flamingo Hotel in Las Vegas. In any event, the three young mobsters helped form the Five Points Gang, graduating from street robberies and other small-time crime into a major NYC bootlegging operation. Moving cases of liquor stood as the most lucrative source of illegal money during the height of Prohibition in the 1920s.

As the Five Points Gang grew in influence, Luciano recognized Lansky's analytical, calculating mind and his penchant for staying behind the scenes. Lansky provided astute strategy sessions while Luciano—himself a combination of street smarts and big thinker—handled the tactics. Their gang quickly transformed into a tiered organization with Lansky its mapmaker.

Lansky's signature expertise involved setting up a method of accounting that satisfied IRS reporting while maintaining a secret, separate ledger to keep track of unreported income. That precise tracking of cash also tended to keep subordinates more honest. Lansky instituted budgeting rules to follow and refined the best methods for washing money via businesses and organizations the Mafia could own or control that gave off the most cash flow. His success in establishing these accountability methods inevitably became a model for all Mafia families and earned him the moniker "The Mob's Accountant."

With Luciano's rise to the top of the Mafia hierarchy in the 1930s, Lansky accordingly wielded enormous power and earned the respect normally reserved for mob bosses. As the families in various major cities became second in power and influence in America only to the U.S. government, Lansky's name would forever be included in the rogues gallery of top Mafia mobsters such as Luciano, Capone, Costello, Genovese, Giancana and Gotti. By its own credo, *La Cosa Nostra* could be composed only of those with Italian descent. As such, the Jewish Lansky could never be a made man. The fact that few other mobsters possessed the moxie to be a capable organizer and planner meant that Lansky's skills benefited the Mafia, and therefore his descent could be accepted and the trust in him indisputable. When he presented a plan of action, everyone already knew Lansky had carefully considered all the ramifications.

While Capone went to the slammer in 1932 and returned in 1939 to Florida a broken and sick man, Lansky remained a part-time resident of South Florida until his death from lung cancer in 1983. Although in his later years he claimed to be retired (as do most aging mobsters), Lansky organized a massive gambling empire from Miami to Palm Beach from the 1930s through the early 1960s that included the involvement of prominent big-time members of organized crime. Lansky also had major interests in casinos in Cuba and London.

Known as "The Little Man," Meyer Lansky in fact became a huge
figure of importance to the Mafia due to his genius for devising
methods to wash money and to skim casino cash. (Federal Bureau
of Investigation)

As it affected Lansky and the rise of the NYC families, in the 1920s the
Mafia street gangs were controlled by Giuseppe Masseria from his home
base in southern Italy. Another Mafioso challenged his authority, leading
to factions for and against Masseria. A parallel internal issue involved the
main influence of traditional leaders who didn't want to deal with anyone
not Italian, versus a newer bloc who would work with non-Italians if they
served the purposes of the Mafia. Luciano headed the latter group, and
amid double-crosses and switched allegiances he whacked Masseria in ca-
hoots with Salvatore Maranzano.

Maranzano moved quickly to organize Mafia families that included his own as well as those of Joe Profaci, Tommy Gagliano, Vincent Mangano, and Luciano. However, in 1931 Maranzano—feeling threatened at the rise of Luciano under his wing—plotted to kill Luciano. Such is the eternal treachery of the criminal world. But that plot backfired when Luciano got tipped off. He struck first, and that was the end of Maranzano and the beginning of the dominant reign of Luciano. After rubbing out Maranzano, Luciano formed the Commission, composed of himself as chairman with NYC members Mangano, Profaci, Gagliano and Joe Bonanno, with the Chicago mob represented by Al Capone and the Buffalo clan by Stefano Maggaddino.

The original family formed by Maranzano became the Bonanno family; Gagliano's became Lucchese; Mangano's became Gambino; Profaci's became Colombo; and Luciano's became Genovese—the infamous five NYC Mafia families. Crime family names often change by way of new leadership due to deaths or incarcerations, while sometimes names remained due to respect for a more powerful or historic don. An example is the Gambino family keeping that name despite proceeding dons of Anastasia and Gotti.

The Commission split up the territories to decrease misunderstandings about jurisdictions, and rules were set in place to handle disputes and hits. Notably, all five families agreed to include South Florida in their purview, meaning they all wanted to keep a foot in the door with the recognized potential for illegal operations in the Sunshine State.

Besides Lansky taking up digs in South Florida in 1929, he also resided at one time or another in Tel Aviv (until expelled by Israel), Havana (until run out of Cuba by Castro), Mafia-run hotels in Las Vegas, and Central Park condos in New York City.

It's a certainty that Lansky crossed paths with Capone in Miami during the span from Scarface's purchase of the Palm Island home until his prison term began in 1932. It's been widely reported that Lansky threw a party at his home the night before the Valentine's Day Massacre, which makes it an interesting coincidence if true. However, Capone didn't need another alibi to prove he was in Miami Beach during those Chicago murders, and being seen chilling with a well-known Mafia associate like Lansky would be illogical for anyone except the flamboyant Capone. At the least they communicated through their henchman or by phone, as there are no known records of law enforcement wiretaps in Miami back then.

Capone and Lansky did have a run-in about who would control the national racetrack wires in the 1930s. The wire service served as a central factor in bookmaking operations around the nation, sending out the results of horseracing tracks soon after each race. The slight delay between the end of a race and a report on which horses won, placed, or showed allowed crooked bookies to past post. Past posting means that bets placed after the outcome has been determined and is known by a bookie or mob betters enables controlling favorable odds to guarantee a profit. To avoid suspicion, past posting isn't commonly done on each race or those races with long odds, but it's exercised enough for whoever is controlling the racetrack wires to rake in millions. Accessing a national wire service alone and making deals with associated bookies became a serious moneymaker.

Enter Moses "Moe" Annenberg, a circulation employee of the *Chicago Tribune,* who became an executive of then media giant Hearst Corporation. Annenberg went on to own and publish titles of his own, including the *Daily Racing Form,* and that would make him the key man in a mobster tug-of-war. To revisit Prohibition, the Mafia—with its extensive political connections—foresaw its repeal and began shifting from bootlegging as the primary income stream to forms of gambling.

Florida's open lack of opposition to Henry Flagler's gambling houses and the proliferation of bolita throughout the state made it clear to the Mafia that South Florida would be an ideal base for gaming operations. That Lansky became a homeowner there in 1929 was likely no coincidence, particularly with the Magic City's proximity to lawless Cuba and the rest of the Caribbean.

Scarface expected Annenberg via his *Daily Racing Form* to help him become the nation's gambling kingpin. Annenberg for sure didn't say no to Capone—a feint most wise—but he harbored second thoughts. It's a certainty that Annenberg knew the mob's pecking order, and in 1929 he secretly approached Lansky about throwing his cards in with Lansky instead of Capone. If Lansky and the established Mafia families wanted to control racetrack bookmaking, the Little Man needed to protect Annenberg from Capone's wrath. No one, not even Chicago's mob boss, dared challenge Lansky's wishes. It's doubtful Lansky even needed Luciano's intervention to quell any temptation by Capone to disembowel Annenberg.

As the Depression set in and Prohibition ended, Lansky and a few other insightful mob members began buying Florida real estate—particularly hotels large enough to host gambling parlors—as well as interests in horse and dog racetracks. The Depression and two major hurricanes in 1926–27 temporarily stalled Florida's land boom. But those with ready cash took advantage. Casino gambling was still illegal in Florida in the early 1930s, and as already indicated, although cops staged raids here and there, the Mafia payoffs and slick high-powered attorneys resulted in few convictions except for lower-level operatives.

Florida legalized slot machines in 1935 and raked in its own share of dinero, but law enforcement—even those agencies not on the take—could not crack down on the immense scope of illegal betting going on practically out in the open. Even when they did conduct raids, thanks to Lansky the cops were clueless about skimming or the scope of investment taking place in Florida by the Mafia.

Moe Annenberg subsequently got nailed in 1939 by the IRS for income tax evasion because law enforcement couldn't convict him for anything else—again, a fact largely attributable to Lansky's spadework. Adding to the lack of mobster crackdowns was the U.S. entry into World War II, when thousands of young men—many from police departments—answered Uncle Sam's call to arms. The nation's attention focused more on the bad deeds of Hirohito and Hitler than on organized crime members.

Even before the war ended in 1945, things were already warm in South Florida. As Capone wasted away in prison, the behind-the-scenes Lansky and others put together a bookmaking syndicate based in South Florida that controlled numerous racetrack betting and gambling parlors. Armed with the permission of the mob, including the Trafficante family in Tampa, gangsters laid their claims for a slice of the illegal gambling pie.

Since we're going to get into the skinny about bookmaking via wire services, let's define terminology that's part of illegal gambling. We're not talking here of bolita tickets being sold on street corners, but of activities based on legitimate competitions such as horse racing, jai alai and greyhound racing. Mutuel betting involves all bets being pooled before a race, and after the winners are determined, a final payout is figured based on odds after the pool is closed, such as just before a race begins. Odds are set based on the chances a handicapper or handicappers judge a race, for example, in what order horses will cross the finish line.

The longer the odds, such as 20 to 1, the more the payout will be if you bet on that horse to win, come in second (place) or come in first, second or third (show). If odds are lower, such as 2 to 1, your chances of that horse winning, placing or showing are higher but the payout will be lower. If someone bets $100 on a horse to win with odds of 2 to 1, the bettor receives his original $100 bet plus $200.

In illegal bookmaking operations, the bookie receives a percentage of the bets (vigorish) and then the remainder is paid to winning bettors. Some bookies can charge as high as 25 percent of the pool in locations that lack other popular forms of legal gambling. For those with gambling fever, it's an adrenaline rush to "beat the odds" now and then at a racetrack. As I'm sure you're aware, there are off-track betting facilities nowadays where one doesn't have to be present. If a syndicate is created with multiple locations that controls the wire service and books bets, the take can be astronomical. And that's exactly what Meyer Lansky did.

On top of bookmaking the gambling parlors offering card and table games and slot machines pulled in huge amounts of cash, and where casino gambling is legal the skim can be substantial if done right. And it was done right because Lansky perfected it. The house also makes money legally in a casino setting with the rake—a small percentage removed from the total bets that goes to the house. That small percentage adds up to large cash flows in a busy casino. Slot machines are similarly set to pay off less than 100 percent of the betting, and the popularity and simplicity of slots for those intimidated by, or unskilled at, other forms of casino gambling mean that slots usually account for a majority of legal profits.

The skim is taking in a gross amount but only reporting part of it; for example, if in a casino's private count room the day's total revenue is $300,000 but only $250,000 is reported. Other ways to cheat the tax man besides skimming are "loose pulls" when unscheduled slot machines are emptied, currency scales or counters are rigged, and, less frequently, armored truck robberies can be staged. Again, Lansky devised methods for under-reporting income that wouldn't cause red flags, which can be the case if too much is skimmed or the reports are unbalanced compared to previous reports; the same applies with businesses used to launder money. Unsophisticated accounting methods and greed usually led to the downfall of skimmers.

Attempts in Florida over the years to legalize full-scale casino gambling have all ended with a statewide vote prohibiting it—usually with those in favor of it residing in South Florida. Meanwhile, most other forms of gambling continue, such as bingo, horse racing, jai alai, low-stakes poker games, and a very active state lottery. There have been many lawsuits challenging Florida's gaming laws, especially by the Seminole tribes versus pari-mutuel operators. Confusing matters at times is that the laws can change instantly per the verdict of a judge, through action by the Florida legislature, or, less frequently, by statewide referenda.

Some of the more notable dates relating to Florida's legal gambling industry:

- 1931, horse and dog racing approved.
- 1935, slot machines legalized due to legal gambling competition in Cuba and New Orleans; two years later this is repealed.
- 1970, bingo legalized.
- 1984, cruise ships taking gamblers to international waters begins (see chapter 4 on Gus Boulis).
- 1986, statewide lottery legalized.
- 1988, Indian Gaming Regulatory Act passes federally, affecting Florida's Seminole tribes in Tampa, Hollywood and Immokalee.
- 1996, poker legalized where pari-mutuel betting is allowed, with increased betting minimums in ensuing years.
- 2004, slot machines allowed at pari-mutuel locations in Miami-Dade and Broward counties.
- 2005, Broward County approves slot machine and Miami-Dade does same in 2008.
- 2010, Seminole tribes given the temporary right to offer slot machines, blackjack and baccarat at seven casinos.
- 2021, a federal court upheld Florida's gaming compact with the Seminoles, establishing that the location of a bet is based on the location of where the bet is placed. That distinction is important in knowing under which legal jurisdiction a bet is made.

Lansky first set up in Broward County in 1935 on the heels of Anthony "Little Augie Pisano" Carfano, a New York City Mafioso under Luciano, who received the green light to open a casino in Miami. Interestingly, Lansky ordered Carfano killed 24 years later because he didn't agree to a meeting with new boss Vito Genovese. Lansky still ran bookmaking operations in and through bookies who had to utilize Moe Annenberg's National Wire Service. The Little Man also made investments in dog and horse racing tracks, including in Broward County such as the Hollywood Kennel Club and Gulf Stream Racetrack as well as Tropical Park Racetrack in Dade County. In the ensuing 15 years, Lansky's ownership interests were estimated at an astonishing 50 establishments.

Aside from Florida casinos blossoming after Prohibition and the popularity of bolita, a major illegal cash cow sprang forth in South Florida in 1944 and exploded in scope after World War II. A massive bookmaking syndicate operated under the incorporated name of "S&G;" but we'll drop the semicolon hereafter, although it was part of the corporate name. S&G

consisted of bookmaking gangsters who decided there was strength in uniting: Eddie Rosenbaum, Jules Levitt, Harry Russell, Charlie Friedman, Sam Cohen and Harold Salvey.

The S&G group pooled money to help finance hotels that provided concession bases, such as at cabanas on the properties for betting on the horse races locally and nationally. At one point those locations numbered as many as 65 in South Florida. Even corner news and cigar stands were controlled by S&G. S&G operatives bribed numerous political officials, prosecutors, judges and police chiefs—most notably Broward Sheriff Walter Clark and Dade Sheriff Jimmy Sullivan—giving casinos and S&G an almost unfettered ability to operate and haul in many millions of dollars per year.

S&G's annual take alone was estimated to be between $40 and $60 million. Clark, a former butcher who served as Broward's sheriff from 1931 to 1950, referred to casinos as "clubs," and as many as 52 operated in his county, some just one-dealer operations and others opulent, fully staffed casinos. Clark and his brother Bob, a Broward deputy sheriff, were part owners of the Broward Novelty Company, which ensured huge income from sales of slot machines and selling bolita tickets. Just what you don't want on the part of a sheriff.

Even a chief of police in Florida during the 1930s and '40s took home chump change, and with mainly males in the workforce—especially those supporting a family—the lure of living the good life often trumped any conscience barriers about being bribed. The same went for all levels of law enforcement and the judiciary, in particular the beat cops. There were honest types aplenty too, but they remained in the background or unable to put a dent in the scale of illegal gambling taking place.

Meyer Lansky tried to keep a low profile, but his reputation preceded him everywhere. Nonetheless, his Mafia connections included overseeing the front men handling the day-to-day S&G operations. Just a few of the establishments out of which S&G managed the bookmaking action included the Roney Plaza Hotel on Miami Beach, Club Boheme at Ocean Drive and Hallandale Beach Boulevard, Colonial Inn just south of Gulfstream Park, Club Greenacres on Pembroke Road, and numerous other properties, including the Mercantile Building, Wofford Hotel, Grand Hotel, Sands Hotel, Boulevard Hotel, Rainbow Grill, and Boca Raton Club.

Interlaced with the clubs in varying capacities were mobsters such as Meyer's brother Jack Lansky, Vincent "Jimmy Blue Eyes" Alo, Joseph "Joe Adonis" Doto, Michael "Trigger Mike" Coppola, and "Minister of the Underworld" Frank Costello. You can bet that all those whose last name ended in a vowel, and whose first and last names were separated by a nickname in quotes, were not dudes you wanted to mess with.

Lansky's first major interest in the income potential of the ponies may have sprouted due to his vision of an expanding bookmaking opportunity per the deal with Moe Annenberg back in 1929 to control the *Daily Racing Form*. As it pertained to casinos, Lansky learned the ropes from Arnold "The Brain" Rothstein, who in 1919 opened the Brook Club in Saratoga Springs, New York, next to its famous racetrack. Existing speakeasies and casinos generally offered dingy, spartan, crowded interiors with few amenities, but Rothstein changed all that to attract more monied gamblers.

The Brook Club featured attractive décor that included plush carpets, European artistry, wide aisles, floor shows and fine food. Lansky, his brother Jake, and Alo mimicked the Brook Club's elegant ambiance by opening the Plantation casino on Hallandale Beach Boulevard. They had partnered with Julian "Potatoes" Kaufman, a rich kid and former Bugs Moran crony. Kaufman—another Chicago mobster on the wrong side of Capone, a la Moe Annenberg—sought and received the protective wing of Lansky in South Florida.

Kaufman had run the Sheridan Wave Club casino in Chicago and moved to Broward County to avoid being whacked by Scarface. He remodeled a farmyard barn into the Plantation, and following its success Lansky and partners soon opened another Hallandale casino at the Colonial Inn just south of Gulfstream Park. Their properties for gambling and bookmaking quickly spread to the It Club on Southeast 28 Street, the Hollywood Yacht Club and others previously listed.

Other gangsters besides Lansky put their irons in the gambling fire. Capone's cronies ran the casino at the Hollywood Country Club. Captain Eugene Knight operated Club Unique on the Intracoastal Waterway. Bill Stewart owned the River View Club in Deerfield Beach that served wealthy guests of the Boca Raton Hotel and Club.

Colonel E. R. "The Colonel" Bradley's Beach Club operated in Palm Beach for nearly 50 years beginning in 1898 and ending just after World War II. Throughout Florida and especially South Florida, anyone wishing to play cards or bet on numbers, spins of roulette wheels, dice, horses, greyhounds, jai alai, or anything else had no trouble finding action. All the operators needed to stay in business consisted of plenty of cash to pay fees (bribes) to law enforcement bigwigs. We return to Bradley later.

One popular hangout for gangsters and visiting celebrities to South

Florida wasn't a casino at all—Joe Sonken's Gold Coast Restaurant and Lounge in Hollywood, mentioned in chapter 4 and involving Gus Boulis. Many deals allegedly took place there between underworld types, and although Sonken also had ties to the Mafia, Lansky seldom if ever visited, as he typically avoided rubbing shoulders at crowded joints with fellow mobsters.

Lansky's ornate gambling properties—like those pioneered by Rothstein and Kaufman—also sported dealers and cigarette/beverage girls in spiffy outfits. High rollers showed their favoritism by keeping the tables and slots busy. While Kaufman represented a pioneer of sorts when it came to stylish gambling houses, he did not live long enough to witness the explosion of casinos and a major bookmaking syndicate in South Florida. Obese, he suffered a heart attack in 1939 and died at the age of 41.

Although Meyer Lansky had become a pariah to law enforcement even before World War II, he helped in the war effort—a fact the government didn't disclose for many years. At that time, Lucky Luciano was in prison on major prostitution charges, so the War Department asked Lansky to meet with his old friend to seek assistance in two ways: to ferret out any saboteurs working as longshoremen who might be feeding info about ship departures from New York Harbor to German submarines waiting offshore, and to provide more detailed maps of Sicily than the Army's obsolete tourism maps.

Known as Operation Underworld, the Mafia hence clamped down on secrecy involving the shipping docks, and the Army could better plan attacks when invading Sicily. This act of assistance gave Lansky temporary chits with the U.S. government and gave Luciano a hugely reduced sentence. According to Sandra Lansky, Meyer's daughter, her father treasured a copy of the signing of the Japanese surrender on the USS *Missouri* given to him by the U.S. Navy.

But some of the post-war glory as it related to the S&G syndicate didn't last forever. They had an estimated 200 bookies doing business through the S&G establishments. Bookies paid S&G up to $150 per week—referred to as "ice money"—to access their network and the Continental Press Service's racing wire. Bets were placed by phone, and the wins/losses per bookie were settled with profits divided 50/50 each month. It proved to be a massive cash cow for all involved.

But here's where Capone's cronies stepped back into the bookmaking picture as the Chicago mob again controlled the wire service. Arthur "Mickey" McBride, then owner of the Cleveland Browns football team and prominent resident of the swank Miami suburb of Coral Gables, owned the Continental Press Service. Reluctantly, in order to keep obtaining instant results of races from all over the country, the S&G was pressured by McBride to make Capone henchman Harry "The Muscle" Russell a partner in S&G.

The party came crashing down on S&G and bookmaking as a syndicate in 1950 due to the Kefauver hearings, and bookies went back to private bets on a smaller scale. The impact of Senator Estes Kefauver and his investigative committee on illegal gambling cannot be overstated, and that is addressed in more detail in an upcoming chapter. But 1950 hardly represented the end of Lansky's escapades. Lansky and company—always playing dodgeball with the law—switched their focus on the casino business to Cuba with the already corrupted dictator Fulgencio Batista as a willing accomplice.

Batista served from 1933 to 1944 as Cuba's president after a coup d'état, and then after eight years of leisure took over the country again from 1952 to 1959 after being backed by the U.S. in a bloodless coup. During both periods of his leadership, the dictator silenced political opponents and enriched himself and his cronies via generous patronage. He fled Cuba in 1959 to avoid certain death at the hands of Fidel Castro, settling in the Dominican Republic and later Portugal. Lansky and the Mafia had to abandon Cuba as well, as the pro-communist Castro nationalized all businesses including hotels and nightclubs.

The Batista relationship became rooted in the late 1940s when Batista agreed with Lansky for the Mafia to obtain licenses and ownership over Cuba's casinos and racetracks when he returned to power in exchange for lucrative kickbacks. The Mafia had already considered Cuba a "soft target" years before when on December 22, 1946, at the Hotel Nacional in Havana, mobsters from across the United States, such as Joe Bonanno, Santo Trafficante Jr., Carlos Marcello, Albert Anastasia, Frank Costello, Joe Adonis, Vito Genovese, Thomas Lucchese, Joe Accardo, Lansky and others converged for a conference. They viewed Cuba and Havana particularly as ripe for their style of lawless businesses.

The Batista connection was like finding a gold mine for the Mafia. Check that; make it a diamond mine. Havana's harbor, with its proximity to Florida, had previously been a handy center for moving liquor and later illegal drugs to Florida for transport to all points north, but with Batista holding the reins of power the Mafia owned major hotel resorts with casinos and racetracks, operating 100 percent in the open. They didn't need

Lansky retired in the 1970s and became a full-time resident of Miami Beach but remained under constant scrutiny by law enforcement agencies until his death in 1983. (Federal Bureau of Investigation)

to skim because the government was the Mafia's partner. For years it was the tightest relationship in history between *La Cosa Nostra* and an independent country, and Luciano and all the Mafia families not only tapped into a huge source of income—they could also vacation sans wives and enjoy booze, women, and beaches to their hearts' content. And there was absolutely nothing the U.S. government or any other entity on earth could do about it.

As noted, Castro killed that party in 1959, and the Mafia took their losses—especially Lansky personally, who lost hotel-casinos such as the Habana Riviera, Montmartre, and Hotel Nacional. The fun was over, and that meant resuming focus on skimming legal casinos in Nevada, as the Kefauver hearings in 1950 and had put the whammy on bookmaking operations and state lawmakers began making it tougher for South Florida casinos to survive even when keeping palms greased.

There is much more about the enormous scope and benefits of the Lansky-Batista partnership that lasted for years, but this book is about mobsters and their activities in Florida. Even so, other chapters have more to say about Lansky and his involvement with other Mafiosi doing business in the Sunshine State.

Lansky spent his last days with wife Teddy and their Shih Tzu dog Bruzzer. Suffering from lung cancer, he still walked Bruzzer when able while under 24/7 surveillance by gendarmes and hounded by paparazzi. He died on January 15, 1983, and is buried in Mount Nebo Cemetery in Miami. It has been estimated that at the height of his power, Lansky's net worth was between $200 and $300 million, but his biographers claim that is a huge exaggeration.

It is true that over the years Lansky gave away much of his money to Jewish charities and causes along with support for first wife Ana, daughter Sandra, and sons Paul and Buddy, the latter afflicted with cerebral palsy since birth and 100 percent dependent on care. Some—including Lansky's daughter Sandra—claim that Lansky hid money in other people's names and transferred millions to various accounts in the early 1970s, such as to Switzerland when the IRS tried to trace his net worth in hopes of bagging him for tax evasion.

Despite all his dealings with ruthless Mafia members and a life of being involved in the dark and grisly world of organized crime, Lanksy was convicted only once in his adult life for illegal gambling, in 1953, and spent just two months in jail. He never expressed remorse for his life, and in fact when once asked if he could have put his organizational expertise to work in a legitimate way, he reportedly smiled and said, "It wouldn't have been as much fun."

7

PATSY & BOBBY

After selling my first security consulting company, I served part-time as executive director of Bonefish & Tarpon Unlimited (BTU, now Bonefish & Tarpon Trust) from 2002 to 2009. Based at Ocean Reef Club, an exclusive private city of millionaires and billionaires in the northern portion of Key Largo, BTU consisted of a board of directors including big-moneyed Ocean Reef residents and saltwater fly-fishing legends such as Stu Apte, Billy Pate, Sandy Moret, Lefty Kreh and Mark Sosin. The theme was to combine the experience of flats fishing experts with scientific knowledge from Florida marine biologists specializing in bonefish and tarpon research.

I coordinated BTU's membership and scientific research, which involved state-of-the-art electronic tagging of tarpon and bonefish. I'd also been a magazine editor for several state and national publications, such as *Florida Sportsman, Sport Fishing* and *Traveling Sportsman,* as well as a radio show host in Miami and the Keys. As such, I dealt at one level or another with numerous boat and tackle manufacturers, outdoor writers, and recreational anglers.

On occasion I'd be confronted by an irate reader with some sort of bone to pick over an article I'd written or something said on the radio show. Such is the lot of a journalist—if I write a nice article about the Apple Pie Association, I'm going to get a nasty letter from the Cherry Pie Association. One day in 2004 or so I received an extraordinarily vulgar verbal barrage at the very outset of a phone call while at my home office in Tampa.

The man identified himself as Bobby Erra and then immediately blurted, "You tell that cocksucker that if I ever catch him anywhere near me on the flats I'll fucking kill him—and I'm not kidding."

What? I nearly hung up, but then curiosity got the better of me. "Who are you and what's your beef?"

"I just read your story about fishing with Billy Pate," Erra growled. The article referred to a BTU fishing-tagging trip to Homosassa—an old Florida Gulf Coast town about an hour's drive north of Tampa that's been considered mecca for saltwater fly fishing for tarpon since the 1980s.

Pate had held the world record on fly for tarpon for nearly 20 years until bested in 2001 off Chassahowitzka, just south of Homosassa. The wealthy Pate, an heir to the Magic Weave Carpet fortune, focused his life entirely on pursuing tarpon records on fly once he retired in the 1960s. Along the way he produced commercial how-to videos about tarpon tactics, one of which involved hiring a helicopter to get aerial footage while he fished off Homosassa. That did *not* go over well with area guides, who charge many hundreds of dollars to take well-heeled clients fly fishing in the hopes of battling tough-fighting, leaping tarpon—especially the prized specimens that exceed 100 pounds.

"That stupid mother fucker ruined the fishing for everyone else on the flats for several days, including me," shouted Erra, explaining that the noise and wind from the chopper chased away all the tarpon. "He didn't even have the courtesy to warn everyone first."

"So why are you calling me about it instead of Billy Pate?" I asked.

"Because assholes like you make Pate out to be a hero when all the guides around Homosassa think he's a self-centered fucking dick," he replied.

I'd had enough of this vulgarian. "I have two words for you, buddy, and they aren't Merry Christmas."

Erra snickered. "Not scared, huh? Well, I doubt if you would say that to my face."

And then, as if turning on a light switch and ignoring the fact he'd just cussed me out, Erra softened his tone. "So, tell me about Bonefish & Tarpon Unlimited, tough guy. Better yet, tell me in person if you've got the balls."

Erra said that on my next jaunt to Key Largo for a BTU meeting, I'd be a luncheon guest at his restaurant in North Miami Beach. I later learned that Erra owned a chain of Italian-themed eateries from Miami to Orlando, each with "moon" in its name; the one in North Miami Beach was called Half Moon, if memory serves me correctly.

With the next executive board meeting of BTU upcoming, I asked around about Bobby Erra. Richard Stanczyk, a longtime friend and owner of Bud 'N' Mary's Marina in Islamorada in the Keys, warned me that he knew Erra from the "cocaine cowboy days" of the 1970s and '80s in Miami. Stanczyk advised, "He's capable of anything—the last time I talked to him he threatened me."

Bobby's dad, Pasquale "Little Patsy" Erra, grew up in New York City as a soldier in the Genovese family and later became its point man for operations in South Florida. (Button Guys of The New York Mafia)

Others told me stories about Erra's Mafia connection through his dad and described his explosive temper. Earle Waters, a veteran fishing guide, said he never knew any mobsters before moving to Homosassa.

"When Bobby Erra showed up to fish our tarpon run each year, I was forewarned about who he was and certainly heard from others about encounters at Homosassa and the Keys," said Waters. "He was hard to avoid at times." Erra would often book a guide for every day during some of the spring and summer months, particularly in May, that being the annual high point for tarpon when they cruise in shallow waters that hug the coastline. That heightened visibility allowed guides to spot the big silvery fish easily and to get their anglers in a position to make casts.

"I knew somebody who went to high school with Erra, and after drag racing in front of the school he got called into the principal's office," Waters said. "Bobby reached across the desk, grabbed the principal's shirt and threatened him. If Bobby had called his dad, Bobby would have had him killed."

Ah yes, his dad. Did you ever notice that sons of Mafia members often followed in the crooked footsteps of their dads? Such was the case of Robert "Bobby" Erra. His dad, Pasquale "Patsy" Erra, moved to Miami in the late 1940s, as did many Mafiosi from northern climates before and after him. Born in 1915 and raised in NYC's precarious Harlem district, Patsy grew up tough enough to become a professional boxer as a bantamweight.

He did well, winning seven of eight bouts, but ran afoul of the law and ended up in prison for a larceny charge in the late 1930s.

At first Patsy pulled some jobs for crew members in various Mafia families, but he really ascended when meeting up with Mike "Trigger Mike" Coppola, a Genovese capo with ties to Lucky Luciano. Coppola and Patsy forged a tight friendship, and Patsy soon moved up as a Genovese soldier in 1949, along with his brother Michael, both proposed by Coppola. They became members of Coppola's crew.

Patsy thereafter moved to Miami Beach, as did Coppola, serving as a bodyguard/henchman and, like all crew members, at times participating in commissioned hits. But Patsy had ambition and wanted more, and Coppola knew it. He let Patsy cavort with members of other families, such as Ray Patriarca, don of the Rhode Island Mafia. While the next chapter chronicles Coppola when he lived in Florida, for now just know that he died in 1966, and Patsy Erra took over all Genovese activities in South Florida.

Some labeled Patsy Erra as the new "Mob Mayor of Miami," which is a bit of an exaggeration, considering the frequent presence of Lansky, Vincent "Jimmy Blue Eyes" Alo, and others with a higher Mafia status. Still, during Patsy's life as a Floridian through the 1960s and until his death in 1973 at the age of only 58, he swung a big club—notwithstanding the indignity of his arrest on gambling charges a year before he died.

Over the years Patsy bought pieces of real estate and stakes in various gambling and bookmaking operations. He also became a partner with Vincent Teriaca in the Dream Bar in the Johnina Hotel at Collins Avenue and 71st Street on Miami Beach. Teriaca, also a Genovese soldier, had previously been arrested on a gambling charge in New York City and ran a major shylocking operation in New Jersey. Besides the Dream Bar, Teriaca watched over South Florida nightclubs owned by fellow New Jersey mobster Angelo "Gyp the Blood" DeCarlo.

Patsy hobnobbed with Alfredo "Freddy Franco" Felice—they lived just a few blocks from each other on Miami Beach. Felice was a Gambino member involved in gambling and narcotics trafficking and who grew up in Patsy's Harlem neighborhood. Felice moved to Miami Beach in 1948 and enjoyed ties to powerful mobsters such as Mike Coppola and the infamous Philadelphia boss Nicodemo "Little Nicky" Scarfo. Felice got nailed in 1953 for a jewel robbery and, like most wise guys, piled up a substantial rap sheet.

Another Mafia pal of Patsy's turned out to be John "Johnny Keys" Simone, a New Jerseyite also associated with the Philadelphia mob as a capo and hit man. Simone became involved in a plot to kill Scarfo, and a contract was put on Simone's head. He ended up being killed in 1980 at age 69 by one of Salvatore "Sammy the Bull" Gravano's crew members. Gravano, the one-time Gambino underboss and feared hit man, felt sorry about having to do the murder after chatting amiably with Simone for hours. Simone did not resist and accepted his fate with honor, a characteristic Gravano valued as being reminiscent of the old guard *Cosa Nostra* members.

Nice bunch of fellows Patsy ran with, right? Birds of a feather flock together, and the acorn doesn't fall far from the tree. Now that we've reviewed Patsy's background, the heritage of his acorn, Bobby, is more understandable. However, unlike his dad, Bobby Erra did perform associate duties but never became a made man. This was probably because he possessed a temper so uncontrollably violent that even mobsters felt unsafe around him.

So why do I dedicate part of a chapter to the son of a Mafia soldier who was a second-generation mobster? Because I got to know him a bit, never becoming tight friends but having in common a background in golf and a love for recreational fishing. I believe the reason Bobby didn't move up the Mafia family ladder was either because Patsy was against it or because Bobby preferred to keep one foot in the criminal side and one foot out. However, that never became clear to me. Made man or not, Bobby became a Miami gangster in his own right, and my connection with him was one of only two personal relationships I developed with those involved in organized crime. The other was Vincent "Jimmy Blue Eyes" Alo (see chapter 10).

Indeed I kept the luncheon date with Erra after the next BTU executive board meeting at Ocean Reef Club. Arriving at the host stand of his restaurant in North Miami Beach, Erra greeted me with a wan smile but a firm handshake, looking burly but spiffy in a dark blue suit. After we shook hands he led me to a table for two. I chose the Steak Marsala on the lunch menu and he did likewise. We then took the measure of each other for a few pregnant seconds, as if in a face-to-face stare in the middle of a boxing ring. I decided to let him speak first.

"I hope you haven't written any more bullshit about Pate," he blurted. Then he gave me that wan smile again. "Let's put that aside for now. I've heard different stories about BTU, and fly fishing for tarpon being my passion, don't know what to believe. Maybe you can fill me in."

Since its inception by big-moneyed Ocean Reef Club flats fishing aficionados in the late 1990s and even to the present day, some fishing guides—

particularly in the Florida Keys and around Homosassa—don't fully trust BTU, and a few have spoken out against it. The main beef centers on who should exercise more input to fisheries managers—guides whose livelihood is earned on the water or a bunch of rich guys on a "feel good" mission to influence regulations regarding bonefish and tarpon and, most recently, permit as well. As BTU's executive director, I spent much of my time mending fences and explaining the non-profit organization's mission to disaffected guides and skeptics like Erra. The biggest misconception was that BTU would use research about where and when bonefish and tarpon congregate, and would tip off the public, thereby ruining various locations familiar to the guides.

As I defined BTU and tried to allay those objections, Erra never broke eye contact. I returned the gaze, not wishing to appear intimidated. He looked every bit the gangster I envisioned: stocky, immaculately groomed, dark hair overly slicked as if coated in motor oil, a confident swagger. I knew Erra wanted to size me up, the mindset of anyone always on the lookout for informants.

As I waxed on about BTU, Erra interrupted. "Where did you go to college?"

I told him the University of Miami on a golf scholarship sponsored by the *Miami Herald.*

"Really?" he asked. "Who was the coach?"

"Doc Heuson," I replied. Heuson was a UM finance professor and coached the golf team for many years, even though he couldn't play a lick himself.

Erra noticeably relaxed and informed me that he had attended UM and had also played on the golf team, a few years before me. He knew darn well that Heuson was the coach, so that little "rat" test turned out negative.

Erra laughed and I asked why. He regaled me about a practice round with the UM golf team at Biltmore Golf Course in Coral Gables when he'd hit an approach shot into a greenside bunker. He flubbed the bunker shot, and Heuson, standing nearby, jokingly chastised him. Erra, enraged at the missed hit, didn't share Heuson's sense of humor about it.

"I threw my sand wedge at the son of a bitch and he ran away like a fucking scared rabbit," laughed Erra. I nodded with my own version of a wan smile. Did I hear just right? This guy assaulted someone—not just anyone, a university professor and his coach—and he thinks it's funny? Different mindset.

Our chat turned back to fishing, and he asked me to describe some of those on the BTU executive board. After I did so, Erra shook his head.

"What's the matter?" I asked.

"Therein lies your credibility problem," he said. "I've been to Ocean Reef Club and mingled with those guys, and you know what? Everything to them is a dick-measuring contest. It's all about who's got the biggest house, the biggest boat, the biggest golf cart, the wife with the biggest tits.

"It's bullshit, they just want to rub shoulders with guides and take credit for what everyone already knows about migration and mating habits. They're going to ruin business for the guides and crowd people on the same flats and fuck it up for people like me."

Countering all that, I stated that many of the board members weren't arrogant and really did want to learn more about tarpon and bonefish to improve the resources. What I didn't say was that there were indeed a few arrogant types on the board, in my opinion.

Erra nodded slowly. "Eh, alright, you seem to be sincere. I don't play golf now, but do love tarpon fishing. So, you know Pate and Apte and all those guys?"

I nodded. Toiling in the magazine editorial trenches for most of the 1990s as managing editor of *Florida Sportsman* and editor of *Sport Fishing*, I often fished with and wrote about many of the well-known record holders, skippers, guides, and expert anglers in the recreational fishing world. Some became friends of mine and still are.

"You already know my opinion of Pate," Erra said. "What about Apte?"

"He and I are close and some say he's the best tarpon angler who ever lived, which I happen to believe."

"I see, and what fly reels does he prefer?" Erra's focus narrowed as he anticipated my answer.

"He owns quite a few brands, but when I produced the four-set video series 'Saltwater Flyfishing from A to Z with Stu Apte' years ago we used Abel Reels," I said.

"Of *course* you did," he roared triumphantly. "I helped design those fucking reels. I know that Steve [Abel, the owner] sent a batch of them to Stu for those videos."

True enough, Abel did exactly that. And yet Erra was still asking me questions to which he already knew the answers. But evidently he was satisfied by now that I wasn't an undercover agent or a snitch looking to become his buddy, and step by step his persona mellowed.

"Okay, tell me about Pflueger."

Al Pflueger Jr. inherited the world's largest taxidermy company when his dad passed away in 1962 and Al Jr. grew the business even further before selling out. His dad also wisely owned valuable property in downtown Miami. From my years of friendship and fishing with Pflueger, I formed the opinion that he's the best all-around angler I've ever seen. Erra chimed in, saying he'd met Pflueger several times and liked his quiet but confident demeanor.

"Okay, okay," Erra said as the waiter removed our plates. His attitude had changed 180 degrees. "You wanna wet a line sometime? Let's see what Stu taught you."

We shook hands. Erra noticed me glancing at his left hand, on which three fingers were missing. He held up the hand and explained that they got chopped off by a boat prop. I've noted that a good many people mixed up in organized crime blame scars and injuries on "accidents." But in Erra's case I tended to believe him as he once raced boats as a thrill sport and owned flats skiffs, so his story about the missing digits may well be true.

I appreciated his offer to go fishing and thanked him for lunch. On the drive back to Tampa I didn't quite know what to think of Erra and figured this was probably the last I'd ever hear from him. That showed how little I knew about the guy. I was to learn that when Erra offers something, it's not just a nicety—he follows through.

Curious about him, I did some research and learned that Erra got arrested in 1991, charged with helping to move shipments of cocaine worth millions of dollars from the Medellin cartel in Colombia to the Bahamas, from where it was then smuggled to Miami on speed boats before being trucked to U.S. points north. On top of that, he also faced a murder conspiracy charge and another for money laundering. Heavy stuff.

Looking down the barrel at perhaps the rest of his life in prison and a cartel informant named Jon Roberts testifying for the government, Erra accepted a plea bargain to all the charges except the murder rap. He received an 11-year sentence.

Some believed that to be a generous deal, considering that Erra may have been involved in much more than the charges mentioned. Also about that time, I read accounts of his dad's Mafia background and that Bobby's college buddy at UM turned out to be Vincent Teriaca's son Gary. Like Bobby, Gary had an inherited predilection for illegal doings, and the two UM grads partnered in various two-bit crimes before getting involved together in the cocaine smuggling ring.

Erra's alleged involvement in murders are tangled affairs. Gary Teriaca's brother was murdered in 1977 by the stepson of Meyer Lansky, and soon thereafter the stepson got taken out. Jon Roberts—whom some described as a teller of tall tales—later claimed that the hit on Lansky's stepson was carried out by a shooter named Ricky Prado and planned by himself, Bobby Erra and Gary Teriaca. In a weird twist, Prado was never charged and instead became a high-ranking CIA agent. Four years later, Teriaca was killed and who did it remained a mystery for 10 years until Alberto San Pedro, another smuggler in the same cocaine ring that brought down Erra—was charged with it.

Pulling fact from fiction and providing an accurate accounting of the endless interconnections between Mafiosi, drug smugglers, murderers and government agents in the 1970s and '80s is no small task. But suffice it to say that Bobby Erra never got convicted for any murders. Learning all that Mafia history about him frightened me a bit, but at the same time I felt intrigued. I wanted to get to know Bobby Erra despite the dangers involved, and that was the first time I realized my infatuation with the Mafia over and above a fascination with related novels and movies.

In the ensuing years I fished with Erra off and on in both the Keys and Homosassa when our travel and schedules coincided. He always called me to line up trips. As we became less formal around each other, I'll never forget an occasion while pausing for lunch amid a day of fishing when I asked about his dad and the Mafia. It was as if someone threw a bucket of cold water on him. He stiffened, put down his sandwich, looked me dead in the eye and said, "Doug, if you want to remain friends, don't ever, *ever* ask me that again."

I didn't. But a year or so later while we sat during a lull in the fishing action in Florida Bay, he stared across the waters and seemed to be in a contemplative mood. He broke the silence and surprised me by expressing regret for his checkered past.

"Obviously I've made some bad decisions in my life," he said. "Who hasn't? I've been hurtful to some people and have my regrets. Being around violence can make anyone violent, and those things come back to haunt you. If I'd been caught doing even one percent of the bad shit I've done, I'd still be in prison or dead. On the other hand, I'm blessed with a family I love and the close friends I do have." That was the first and last time he reflected on his past to me.

I did witness his famous temper on two occasions. The first occurred after a hot day on the flats pursing bonefish. We swilled cocktails at the bar

Bobby Erra readies himself in a casting platform on the bow of a skiff. Erra and the author shared a mutual fondness for fishing. (Dean Butler)

counter at Whale Harbor Marina in Islamorada. A man sitting on a bar-stool across from us said something to the bartender, a woman Erra knew, that made her frown. When she came near us, Erra asked what was wrong and she said the guy said something "inappropriate" to her.

Erra walked over to the man, clenched his hair in a vice grip (obviously with his right hand!) and flung him backward off the stool. The man got up as if to fight—he was tall and in his 30s—but the snarling Erra shouted, "Come on motherfucker, give me an excuse to kill you."

I could see the spittle spewing out of Erra's mouth, his thumb and fore-finger in the shape of a gun pointed at the man's head. The bewildered guy promptly exited the bar and practically fell down the steps leading to the parking lot. Erra climbed back on his stool as if nothing happened, looked at me and said, "Can you believe that last goddamn bonefish didn't eat my fly?"

On another outing on the flats west of Long Key, a man and woman on a Yamaha Waverunner came barreling toward us at full speed.

"Fucking bastards," Erra shouted as loud as he could. He fired up the engine on our boat and hailed them down. They stopped briefly to see what was up, oblivious about both their inconsiderate behavior and impending danger. As we drew close, Erra opened the ice chest and started hurling soda cans at the couple, narrowly missing them.

They blasted off, with Erra shouting every four-letter word known to man even though they couldn't hear anything. Regaining his composure, Erra's breathing returned to normal, and he smiled at me. "Lucky for them I'm in a good mood," he cracked.

But those were isolated incidents. I'd heard rumors that merely missing a hook-up or losing a fish in mid-battle would send Erra into a tizzy. But all anglers mutter when such things happen, and other than uttering a few choice words, he took such disappointments in stride. Maybe after pissing off so many fellow anglers and guides in past years, he finally mellowed out some.

Another problem associated with fishing with Erra involved painfully watching him trying to play a large fish when handicapped with a lame left hand. He went through a myriad of accommodations trying to pump and wind with his mangled hand and take in line with the right hand on the reel, a problem other anglers needn't worry about. After he failed to best a fish one day, I tried to commiserate about how frustrating it must be for him. His explanation made perfect sense.

"I look at it this way, Doug—it's better for me to take out my anger issues on a fish rather than a human," he said. "Believe me, I know my faults. Don't feel sorry for me. I love the challenge and do this because when I catch a prized fish with basically one hand, it's something few others can accomplish."

He was right about that. Although Bobby Erra at times participated in an underworld life alien to me and despite his checkered reputation, I grew to like him. He was genuine, unapologetic, rough at times, but also extremely gentlemanly when his feathers weren't ruffled. Erra wouldn't let me pick up a check or even chip in for food, drinks or gas. He seemed to run a successful restaurant chain and referred to his employees as "my boys." But despite our enjoyable days together, it never got past a certain stage and he never invited me to his home or to meet his family. Then again, I didn't invite him home either.

He specifically asked me not to take pictures of him or even mention him in any of my articles. At first I figured that the fact of my not being "in the life" held him back a bit, but he finally said the reason was that he didn't want anyone else to know where he went or what he did.

"My ego doesn't need to be stroked, and I don't want publicity like Pate and those guys," he said. So be it. I reveal my relationship with him publicly now only because in 2016 Robert "Bobby" Louis Erra succumbed to brain cancer at the age of 71 at his home in Hollywood, Florida. He left behind his wife and two children as well as a brother and two sisters.

More than a few people likely uttered a sigh of relief upon hearing the news of his demise. Understood, but I caught some glimpses of his good side and still think about him often.

8

CONSULTING CONNECTIONS

A few years after graduating from the University of Miami in 1974, I answered an ad in the *Miami Herald* for a "Troubleshooter/Investigator." It turned out to be a security company hiring undercover agents whose job involved going to work for the company's industrial clients as if a regular employee. The idea was to put someone in the client's work force secretly to mingle with employees and to report on malpractices, theft, drug use and job performance. Only the top executive of the client company would know the identity and purpose of the agent.

My dad had served as an intelligence officer after his flying days in the Air Force, so evidently his interest in covert affairs rubbed off on me. I became quite adept as a UC, the industry abbreviation for an undercover agent or operative. I soon came out of the field after several assignments to supervise other UCs and hopped from this security contract firm to another before working for Marriott Security Systems, a division of the Marriott Corporation. I was Director of Investigations, overseeing UC agents internationally in Marriott's hotels, restaurants, and at that time its in-flight catering division for the airlines.

As a profit-making division of Marriott, we also took on outside clients with services such as polygraph testing, surveillance, undercover and mystery shopping. While I wasn't involved in polygraph testing at that time, I did oversee all the investigative services. Unlike a UC agent who poses as a regular employee, a mystery shopper—also known as a spotter, secret shopper, or simply a shopper—poses as a regular customer and reports on the level of service, attitudes, cash or credit transactions, quality of food and drink if a restaurant/bar setting, etc. Clients ranged from retail stores, airlines, warehouses, and banks to restaurants, fast food chains, hotel chains, nightclubs, cruise lines, car dealerships and on and on.

After leaving Marriott to start my own company in 1980, I opened a shopping division and became a polygraph examiner and instructor. In Florida to be a polygraph examiner, one must complete an extensive train-

Mystery shopping services supplied by the author's security consulting firm provided access to owners of bars, lounges and clubs, hotels, cruise lines and casinos. (Kelly S. Kelly)

ing course approved by the Division of Licensing. After that an examiner can conduct polygraph tests as an apprentice for a year to become a fully licensed sponsoring examiner. The instructional course covered the intricacies of a polygraph instrument, question formation, techniques of interviewing, legal restrictions, testifying in court, how to interpret the polygraph chart reactions, observing actual exams being conducted, etc. In my case it involved being in a class eight hours a day, five days a week for six weeks. After graduating from the course, you then had to pass a written test administered by an examiner for whom you didn't work.

At that time polygraph testing was in extensive use commercially to screen prospective applicants before employment and to pinpoint those involved in malpractices and dishonesty. Sometimes a polygraph test was used for individuals who wanted to see if a spouse was faithful. Whether one agrees with the use of polygraph testing or not, at that time my company quickly expanded from one office in Hialeah to two others—one in South Miami and the other in Key Largo—and I kept six examiners busy.

Due to national union pressure, nowadays only specific-use exams are allowed for businesses and individuals, while law enforcement agencies can still use polygraph testing to screen those applying for jobs.

Many security firms existed in Miami offering security guards, mystery shopping services, polygraph testing, background checks, undercover investigations, and surveillance. I did all that too except guard services, but I wanted to provide something few other security firms did: technical surveillance countermeasures, better known as eavesdropping detection or debugging sweeps. I took courses offered by reputable national sweep firms and gear manufacturers. I also served occasionally as an apprentice tech for a leading expert in the field with prior governmental experience. That helped me accumulate the necessary know-how as well as the latest technical equipment—a cost of about $50,000—to perform professional sweep services.

The sweep training and gear allowed me to locate clandestine transmitters, telephone taps, hidden microphones and video cameras, and any

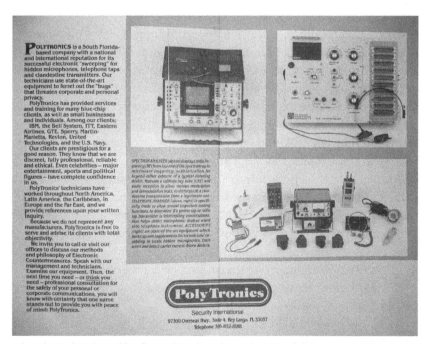

A brochure distributed by the author that showed some of the gear used to locate clandestine transmitters—a service in high demand during the 1980s and '90s. (Kelly S. Kelly)

other listening devices in homes, offices, cars and airplanes. I soon began teaching introductory and advanced seminars for internal security divisions of companies such as AT&T, Martin-Marietta, Sperry, Revlon, the U.S. Navy, UPS, Texaco, an NFL team, and scores of Fortune 500 companies. The money was good, with an average sweep fee of $500 per room and a minimum charge of $2,500 paid in advance. For a party to shell out a few thousand dollars to find out if their conversations are being overheard by a competitor, spouse, foreign government or the law can be a huge bargain if a listening device is discovered. If nothing is found at least the client has peace of mind about the security of communications.

Besides direct mail marketing, word spread throughout various industries about my company. I also wrote articles about sweeps for the American Society for Industrial Security's *Security Management* magazine. Security directors for companies large and small were ASIS members, as were private firms. My company was originally called Deception Control of Miami, but I changed its name to Polytronics International after buying out my partner on a friendly basis. My client base grew for law firms, unions, corporate execs and celebrities.

With the three offices and 17 employees, I stopped taking on more clients. Well, almost. It's hard to talk about bad guys driven by greed when the almighty dollar at times made me take leave of my better senses. Throw in being star struck and having a penchant for overwork, and resistance proved fruitless. Case in point: In late 1983 I received a call from someone who said he worked for Frank Sinatra and was inquiring about my service of "finding bugs." Would I be willing to sweep Sinatra's home in Palm Springs to check it out? Hell yes, I answered.

A week later I was shown into Sinatra's Rancho Mirage residence and led to the pool area. He stepped up the ladder dripping wet and in swimming trunks. I was taken aback at how skinny and gaunt he looked, and I tried not to appear surprised. It did make me appreciate how body padding, elevator shoes, toupees, and makeup can affect one's appearance.

I started babbling about being a fan, and he cut me off cold.

"Listen, I didn't fly you out here for three grand to discuss my career. Let's just cut to the chase, okay pal?"

I asked why he thought his conversations might be compromised and he frowned.

"That's none of your goddam business. Just do whatever you usually do to see if I'm bugged."

I spent hours sweeping his rooms and found no signs of listening devices. I told him so, and for the first time he softened a bit. He seemed intrigued by my gear and asked how the measuring devices worked, saying he was a bit of a gadget freak.

Sinatra mentioned a concern voiced by his security detail that dishonest techs sometimes pretend to find a device just to inspire future business. He thanked me for being honest—although I'm not sure how he'd have felt if I'd found something—and said he'd refer some friends to me.

Ol' Blue Eyes made good on his word. A few months later I did a sweep of Dean Martin's home office in Beverly Hills. In contrast to Sinatra, Dino couldn't have been more down to earth and friendly. I found no evidence of eavesdropping at his place either. After telling him the news, Martin nodded with a smile and said he didn't think there would be. "My friggin' life is an open book," he said, and added that he only agreed to the sweep at Sinatra's insistence.

I also later did a sweep for Bob Hope at his hotel suite at the Savoy Hotel in London, but I never met him. There was nothing awry there either, and I wondered why he would go to such an expense. Then again, he could certainly afford it. It disappointed me that Hope was doing a performance during my presence and one of his staff members—a masseur who accompanied him everywhere—served as my contact.

I did find devices at the family home of President Ferdinand Marcos of the Philippines. And yes, I witnessed a massive room (not a mere closet) jampacked with his wife Imelda's shoes. His reaction surprised me when I informed him about the discovery of a microphone behind the headboard in his bedroom and a tracking device attached under the bumper of his limo. Marcos didn't seem perturbed at all, which caused me to think either he already knew of their presence or he was the world's greatest poker player.

The typical drill when I did find a listening device entailed taking the client to a safe zone away from any buildings or cars and mentioning the device's type and location. At that point he or she can leave it there and feed it false information, remove it, or report it to law enforcement. To my knowledge, no one ever did the latter. Bugs or mics never reveal who planted them, and therefore an eavesdropper's identity is usually unknown; it's impossible to know if it belongs to the FBI, CIA, DEA, state or local law enforcement, a competitor, a foe, or a spouse.

The sweep of Sinatra's Palm Springs home wasn't the last I heard from him. Another of his staffers called with a request for me to fly to L.A. and administer to Sinatra a polygraph test to prove to his wife Barbara that he was a faithful hubby. The intimation was that he needed the report to state that he truthfully answered no to the question, "Have you ever engaged in any sexual activity with anyone other than your wife Barbara while married to her?"

In fact, the fellow said, I could just skip all the time and trouble of flying out there by sending a report to that effect, for which I'd get paid my fee and expenses, as if I'd done the test. I advised that it would be best to find an examiner in L.A., and I reminded him that Sinatra had admired my honesty regarding the sweep I'd performed. The staffer laughed heartily.

"Yeah, I know about that and I don't blame you, buddy," he said. "He [Sinatra] doesn't like to be told no, but I think it's a bad idea too. Don't worry, he didn't mention you doing the test, I just thought I'd check first with you. I'll line up somebody else out here, but from one PI to another, your integrity is appreciated."

I thanked him for the compliment, but that didn't take away my tinge of guilt. To be honest, at times my decisions relating to security work for certain parties fell into a gray area. By that I mean that I might be a trifle suspicious about a guy with a $3 million home, two Ferraris, a private jet, a yacht, and a girlfriend one-third his age as to how he came about such good fortune. But as stated previously, I never asked, and even if I had asked, a person on the wrong side of the law was unlikely to admit it. My services were legal, I did nothing illegal, and if I didn't perform the work, someone else would. In any event, that's how I rationalized doing sweeps for clients I suspected of ill-gotten gains.

The reason I bring up Sinatra is not to namedrop but because his referrals may have extended beyond his Hollywood pals. In the early 1980s I'd sent out a local mailing about mystery shopping to South Florida restaurant and bar owners. One of those responding was Al Malnik, a dashing, aggressive attorney and the co-owner of a high-profile and ritzy club on Miami Beach called The Forge. Rumor had it that Malnik was a protégé of Meyer Lansky. He never denied their connection and friendship, but Malnik always maintained no Mafia involvement himself—a denial many considered dubious. Years later I learned more about Malnik, particularly regarding his close relationship with Sinatra, Dean Martin and other Rat Pack pals. Connecting the dots further, Sinatra rubbed shoulders his entire career with Mafiosi, including Chicago boss Sam Giancana.

I had no qualms either about doing mystery shoppings at The Forge, and even back then I had Mafia fever. At the same time, I had to be careful when it came to taking on sweep clients. The reason is that if law enforcement learned I was locating listening devices they planted, they could pass the word that I was really working for the cops. Plus, I never intentionally wanted to work for the bad guys against the good guys. I know it happened, but that's due to purposeful ignorance—not asking questions about what line of work they're in.

Sometimes you end up doing work for a questionable entity after doing the job. An example of how one can be fooled by appearances occurred one day in 1986. A gentleman in business attire carrying an attaché case visited my office unannounced and asked our receptionist if he could see me. I agreed. He provided a business card showing he was an attorney and said he represented a client who wanted to buy a small private airplane.

No problem there. I'd swept airplanes before, searching for transponders—devices that send out a signal that can be tracked. I suspected the obvious (that he was likely a drug dealer) but gave him the benefit of the doubt. Red flag number one.

I asked where the airplane was located. Great Inagua, he replied, an island at the south end of the Bahamas chain. Red flag number two. But he assured me all was legit; his client just didn't want to buy an airplane that might have been used to haul illegal drugs. Okay, that sounded reasonable. I had him sign an agreement, as I did with all clients, that it was understood my service was legal and that he or she was not involved in any illegal activities. (Worthless in court but better than nothing.) Even so, Miami in the 1980s was rife with cocaine cowboys, and the use of private airplanes to smuggle drugs had already become legendary.

We agreed on a price; customers always paid up front, including estimated expenses. On a weekend day, I and a tech who spoke Spanish and helped me perform the sweeps climbed aboard a twin-engined plane at an executive airport in Miami and flew southeast for hours upon hours until finally coming in for a landing at Great Inagua. I told my client after seeing the runway that if the Bahamian customs folks wanted to inspect my equipment, I was fine with that. His reply: They won't even leave their chairs in the hanger building. Red flag number three.

The "small private airplane" turned out to be a DC-3, the kind requiring a flight of steps to board. The plane had no seats, only plywood slats running throughout the passenger area with the odor of marijuana residue so strong that we practically choked. By this stage I'd run out of red flags and realized I should have exercised better judgment, especially with a wife and two small children at home.

We checked out the plane and a pilot took it airborne in case of altitude-activated transponders. We found two of them.

OMG, I was thinking. If the DEA or another agency was surveilling Great Inagua, I knew our goose would be cooked as we'd be considered drug conspirators. On the flight back to Miami not a word was spoken, but I worried that we might get dropped off somewhere over the Gulf Stream, or fellows would be shoving badges in our faces back at the Miami airport. Fortunately, we landed in one piece late that night, but needless to say I turned down this client when he wanted another sweep on yet another plane. I'm careless on occasion, but not that occasion.

I turned down numerous jobs that I knew for sure weren't legal. One included a request that I rent a room at a Holiday Inn on Brickell Avenue in Miami next to a room where a rival drug gang was ensconced. I explained to the caller that firstly, if his phone was tapped our conversation was already compromised, and secondly that it's against the law in the United States to plant a device or to eavesdrop without a court order. In Florida it's also a two-party consent, meaning all those engaged in the conversation must approve it being overheard or recorded. On another occasion a fellow representing a biker gang wanted me to do sweeps and I turned that down.

The most notorious sweep I ever did was for Eastern Airlines at their headquarters at Miami International Airport in the mid-1980s. We discovered a transmitter in the office of then Eastern President Frank Borman and another in the conference room. At the time, Eastern was embroiled in a major contract dispute with the Machinists Union. Eastern suspected the bugs were planted by the machinists, and the machinists claimed they were planted by Eastern as a ruse. The whole mess ended up as a big story in the *Miami Herald*. I suggested to Borman that he feed false information into the bugs to set up a fake meeting, to see if it was surveilled by the eavesdropper. It would require a surveillance on a possible surveillance! However, right after saying that, I also forewarned Borman that whoever did plant the devices had by then already seen the press coverage about it and would likely be lying low for a while. So he removed the bugs and turned them over to the police. As it turned out, to this day no one knows who the perpetrators were.

I'm sure that on some occasions those calling to see if I'd plant a listening device were state licensing investigators or law enforcement agents. I held a state PI agency license, a personal PI license, and a certified polygraph examiner certificate and a growing family. I wasn't going to throw all that away by doing something illegal. An even bigger motivating factor involved avoidance of pain or death if viewed as a double-crosser. True, I often swept the offices, homes, cars and planes of people who seemed mighty young to be that rich, and did polygraph tests and mystery shoppings for hundreds of clients. I'm certain some of them were bad apples. But that was no different than the practices of thousands of security consulting firms throughout Florida, the U.S. and the world.

While I didn't want to work for the bad guys, I stayed in my lane when it came to working with law enforcement, particularly as it involved the violent world of drug trafficking in Miami. That mental block came about when I first started in the security field as an undercover investigator. I was posing as a janitor at a company that provided real estate maps, and after a few weeks a scrawny guy—let's call him Amos—approached me and asked what I thought about recreational drugs. I replied that some friends did coke but I hadn't tried it yet.

"We gotta fix that, man," he said, his smile revealing two gold teeth.

He invited me to join him and two other employees in the parking lot after work. A joint was passed around, and Amos wanted to know if I might like to score some coke and even sell some to my friends. I agreed. We made a deal for a small amount at first—$200—to see if we'd both be happy with it. We'd meet a few days hence in the company parking lot. Amos advised that after first getting the cash from me he'd go pick up the coke.

After work I reported this to Rex Smith, my supervisor—a former cop and Secret Service agent—at Management Safeguards, for which I worked as a UC. Smith phoned the client to ask if he'd like to fire Amos or have him busted. The client wanted to make an example of Amos, so Smith advised such to a contact of his in Vice at the Miami Police Department. A meeting was arranged in our office on Biscayne Boulevard. A narc showed up at the arranged time looking every bit like a druggy, with unbuttoned shirt, gold chains, a Rolex watch, tattoos and slicked-back hair. After a long discussion, he laid out the plan.

"We'll give you the $200, which we'll mark. Pass Amos the money in the parking lot where you guys have been smoking so we can observe it as we'll be staking it out. We'll follow him to the source where he's picking up the coke so we can later bust his source too. The cash and the coke will be seized at the same time and becomes an unbroken chain of evidence. You'll both be arrested and of course he'll go to jail, and you'll walk away."

He further advised that at night when the company was closed, he'd scope out the best place to hide to get pictures and video. I told him about a thicket of bushes adjacent to the parking lot. I also voiced displeasure at the plan because it would mean not only my leaving that client job but that Amos would probably put two and two together. At that point the plan had been put in motion, so they talked me into going through with it. Yeah, sure, it wasn't their safety at stake and I wasn't being paid enough to get directly involved with busting drug dealers.

The day came for the buy. Amos, sitting at his workstation in the building, waved upon sighting me. We walked back to the parking lot and I gave Amos the money. Suddenly the nearby bushes shook.

"What the hell was that?" I wondered, knowing full well it must have been a clumsy narc. Birds flushed into the air, but it drew quiet and luckily Amos shrugged it off. He got into his car and just started to drive out of the circular parking lot and immediately another car abruptly moved directly behind him. Amos saw that in his rear-view mirror and instead of driving out of the lot he stayed in the circle. I watched in dumbfounded awe as the car behind him kept following closely, both cars going around and around in the lot.

But that's not the end of the story. At that moment a helicopter that had been heard in the distance suddenly appeared directly overhead, and dust from the unpaved parking lot clouded the air.

I'm thinking, "You gotta be shittin' me."

Amos re-parked his car, and as he and I scurried to the door and into the building, I put on an act that would make Pacino proud. "I think someone ratted us out," I shouted to Amos.

"Yeah, tell me about it," Amos said. "Here, take the money back. Nuthin' went down, so we can't get busted."

I didn't blow my cover despite the Three Stooges act by Miami Vice. That UC assignment came to an end a few days later, and the client eventually got rid of Amos and his drug-tooting pals on some sort of technicality. I of course realized that that one bumbling incident didn't represent the competence of the Miami Police Department, but it sure didn't impress me.

I did catch the wrath of the CIA one time though. Two agents paid me a visit. At that time they had an office in Coral Gables, the only other domestic office outside their headquarters in Langley, Virginia. They were not very friendly.

"You're interfering with the security of the United States," said one. "You took something you shouldn't have in Kingston."

A month prior I'd been in Kingston, Jamaica, for a sweep at a company's office building. I found a transmitter above the drop-ceiling tile of the CEO and another in the conference room. The client removed them, and I figured that was that.

"Do you realize how much time and trouble it took to plant those items?" said the other agent, his face gruff.

"What do you mean by 'items?'" I queried.

"You know damn well what we mean. That company you visited is one of the front businesses for the Mafia and drug cartels in the Caribbean. Because of that, you're going to have to furnish us with a list of any sweeps you're doing outside the U.S. so we can temporarily remove whatever might be ours and we'll then put them back after you're gone."

I pointed at the camera conspicuously mounted in a corner of the ceiling. "Be careful what you say and do."

That softened him a bit. "We're not threatening you, sir, but the interests of the U.S. government come before yours."

"I can't divulge the names of clients—it would be a breach of confidentiality," I stated firmly. "No one would ever hire me if they knew I was tipping off the feds. Besides, everyone has a right to ensure their own privacy, and I'm acting legally as their security consultant."

They kept staring, so I posed a question to which I already knew the answer. "Do you obtain court orders to install phone taps or bugs?"

"Of course not. Our purview involves foreign intelligence outside the U.S."

"Then here's the only thing I'll agree to: You guys give me a list of all the foreign places you have listening devices, and if I get a job involving one of those locations, I'll notify you."

They both smirked. "You know goddamn well we can't do that," one of them said.

"I know, so we have a stalemate. If you don't like it, take me to court." Tight-lipped, they brusquely left without saying another word. I notified a contact at Langley to put the confrontation on record and was told not to worry about it, but then received a lecture on the planning time, trouble, and expense that goes into planting listening devices.

I'm sure the CIA installed new bugs at my Kingston client's offices, and I always told clients that my sweeps could only verify the status of any eavesdropping devices as of that same day. But they are on heightened alert if in fact I find them on my visit. As already mentioned, no one chisels on a device the name of the party who planted it. I have no way of knowing if a client has a court order by law enforcement to bug the premises, or is a target of our intelligence services, or simply has a jealous spouse.

I did enjoy the rare privilege of chatting with a U.S. congressman about the presence of *Cosa Nostra* and drug cartels in Florida. Soon after takeoff on a flight in August 1987 from Dulles International Airport in Washington D.C. to Miami, I noted Dante Fascell sitting behind me. No one was in the aisle seat with him, so I turned around and said hello.

Fascell (pronounced Fuh-SELL) served a district that covered the mid- to southern half of Miami-Dade from 1954 until 1993—an impressive stretch of nearly 40 years. He recognized me as the campaign director of one of his prior Republican opponents. Short, stocky and not the handsomest man in Miami, he made up for it by forming close alliances with constituents. Fascell always treated political opponents in a magnanimous and affable manner, a trait sadly missing in today's partisan rhetoric.

He invited me to sit next to him, much to my delight. I asked Fascell why he wasn't sitting in the first-class section. "I usually fly coach," he answered. "It saves taxpayers' money, and if the flight isn't full the airlines sometimes give me a seat with some elbow room."

Fascell and I mused about Florida's horrific law enforcement challenges in the past decade. He expressed exasperation about the status of organized crime, particularly in South Florida. "It's out of control," he said, shaking his head. "Jewish, Irish, Cuban, Mexican, Puerto Rican, Colombian and Haitian gangs—and they all have territorial fights. The only group that seems to keep a lid on the violence is—believe it or not—the Mafia. They're not as prominent as in years past, but they're involved in drug trafficking and operate local businesses to wash money."

Fascell said there was so much cash being made by cocaine cowboys that they couldn't even keep up with counting the money. He remarked about constantly requesting various law enforcement agencies to intervene but said they all had limited resources and different priorities.

"Now and again, there are drug seizures at the airport or on the water or by the Coast Guard and arrests made, but there's little or no cross-communication [between the agencies] because things are happening so fast at times," Fascell said.

"Despite local, state and federal task forces, it's still not enough. It's dangerous out there if someone is in the wrong place at the wrong time."

Fascell referenced a shootout just months before in Miami when two FBI agents were killed in a gun battle with two bank robbers, and he also mentioned the 1979 afternoon shootout by cocaine cowboys at a Miami mall.

On the rest of the flight I pondered how Miami would ever recover from its tarnished reputation as the world's Grand Central Station for drug trafficking. And just how did the Mafia change from being an organization that eschewed drugs to being an active participant? I'd soon get an up-close look at that world with a new mystery shopping client.

9

MUTINY IN MIAMI

Standing with a drink and casually observing a blackjack table at a smoke-choked casino in Panama, I eventually noted that the guy sitting at first base was conspiring with a beautiful Asian woman seated at seventh base. When one of those players was dealt a good hand like a 19 or 20, the player at the opposite end of the table would distract the dealer. For example, if her accomplice received a likely winning hand, she'd exchange flirtatious comments with the dealer, and in that split second her accomplice inconspicuously capped his bet. If dealt a probable bust hand like a 16, he'd pinch his bet while again she distracted the dealer.

Lacking the feminine charms of his lady cohort, the man had to be more inventive for it to work in reverse, such as asking the dealer a question or requesting he summon a bar server while his accomplice capped or pinched a bet.

In gambling parlance, capping (adding to) a bet and pinching (lessening) a bet is a clear case of cheating the casino. It's usually easier to accomplish with young, inexperienced dealers in small-town casinos with few cameras around and lax pit and security personnel. I'd been hired by the casino owner to stay at the hotel as a regular tourist and perform a mystery shopping, not only to detect cheating at the tables but also to provide an evaluation of hotel and bar service.

First off, my client's dealers didn't know how to shuffle properly. Worse, they sometimes made mistakes such as underpayments or overpayments. On occasion players had to instruct them on the correct payouts. Tips were going into dealers' pockets at times rather than into the cash slot boxes.

In this case my client involved a casino run by a henchman of Manuel Noriega, the Panamanian dictator at that time. Similar cheating was taking place at the roulette table, with past posting occurring. Bartenders were sliding free drinks to single women and table servers swung checks—presenting the same check previously paid for drinks costing the same, and the difference not going into the register till.

That latter trick usually indicates collusion with a bartender. The tip container at the bar was often the repository for drink payments. Prostitutes openly worked the lounge and some of them looked to be barely past puberty.

I struggled to keep up with the mental notetaking, which later took place with pen and paper in a locked bathroom stall. The employees must have thought I had a urinary infection. When off premises after my weekend stay I provided the client with an oral report, to which he nodded nonchalantly.

"Good, very good. I must tell them to be less obvious."

And then I got it. The casino was using shills—fake players—to siphon money from the tables as another means of skimming. Some of the dealers and bartenders were probably doing some skimming of their own. The so-called floor security personnel appeared to be barely out of high school, and I'm sure the casino hired them on purpose due to their naïvete.

It also became obvious that the casino used me to pretend they were policing themselves. I have no doubt that my reports were being heavily redacted or falsified. All these skimming games wouldn't escape the scrutiny of any seasoned casino player, much less a security consultant. Fortunately, most casinos—even if engaged in backroom skimming—sincerely want to catch dishonest players and employees.

My security company's mystery shopping division exploded in the 1980s, outpacing our polygraph and sweep biz in growth if not as lucrative. It grew to the point that in just a year I hired a full-time mystery shopping manager and employed two crews of shoppers. While 90 percent of our business was in Florida, we occasionally covered out-of-state clients.

Due to the wide variety of businesses desiring an objective report from the point of view of a customer (managers often provided owners with self-serving babble), our client base varied greatly, but without doubt the bread and butter entailed bar shopping. It required well-trained shoppers who could inconspicuously make observations while blending in with those patronizing their businesses, meaning a matching of ages, genders, and sometimes race or language.

Some might figure that type of matchmaking is prejudicial, and they would be right. Not because of racism, but because you shouldn't send a shopper to a Latino bar who doesn't speak Spanish or an older person to an establishment catering to younger people. A shopper who doesn't fit in sticks out like a sore thumb and becomes less likely to spot any malpractice or dishonesty if it exists.

Burton Goldberg operated the Mutiny Hotel in Coconut Grove (the tall building at rear), which served as a raucous playground for the glorious and notorious during the Cocaine Cowboys era in Miami. (HistoryMiami Museum)

The most infamous of my mystery shopping clients besides The Forge and cruise lines was far and away the Mutiny at Sailboat Bay in Miami's chic Coconut Grove district. Already the late 1960s haunt of hippies and potheads, Coconut Grove offered groovy bars and quaint head shops bordering Miami's glistening bay featuring scores of moored sailboats.

Burton Goldberg owned the Mutiny and rightly figured that a luxurious private 130-room hotel and club catering to well-heeled locals and jetsetters—and never mind how they got their bread—would be a big hit. Little did he know that what he started in 1969 would grow into the coolest and most controversial club in Miami's history.

As is widely known, Miami's so-called underground drug culture boomed in the 1970s and '80s. The town was the epicenter of drama, with gang violence, murders and riots, yet nothing seemed to stop the crowds of tourists and excitement seekers. The Mutiny Club became the "in" place for visiting Hollywood actors, recording artists, con artists, international spies and politicians, all mixing shoulder-to-shoulder with Mafiosi, drug lords and coke-sniffing men and women.

Responding to one of my mystery shopping marketing letters, I received a memorable call from Goldberg in the early 1980s.

"If you want my business, get your fucking ass over here and let's talk."

Who speaks like that to people they've never met? Taken aback, I wrote that down on my daily to-do pad. Hmm, I thought, one day that will be a fitting quote in a book. In any event, hungry for business and familiar with vulgar clients, I arranged a meet-up with him.

Goldberg impressed me, but not in a good way. He came across as a hard-driven, cutthroat type with bouncy thick eyebrows and an overly forceful voice. I'd encountered potential clients when on sales calls who I envisioned might be more trouble than they were worth, and he fell into that category. He was an authority on alternative medicine, a subject he sometimes launched into, to the point that I'd wonder when he would finally shut up so I could quit patronizingly nodding my head. He must have been onto something, however, as years later I would barely survive lung and colon cancer while he lived to the age of 90.

None of the warning signs about Goldberg deterred me. As a Miamian I'd already heard plenty about the members-only Mutiny Club and often drove by it on South Bayshore Drive, wondering about the goings-on inside. Rumors ran amok about drug deals, conspiracies being hatched, cases of high-priced champagne flowing like water, and sex binges aplenty. No commoners would be found among the clientele, with valets being handed the keys to Lamborghinis and Ferraris. I'd soon discover that those rumors were true as the Mutiny Club presented a menagerie of characters rivaling the bar scene in Star Wars.

At our first meeting in his penthouse atop the Mutiny Hotel, I was in my mid-30s and wearing a Brooks Brothers vested jacket and tie with patent-leather shoes.

"You're the right age," he said, glancing me up and down, "but you look like a pussy. Come in here with a jacket but no tie, unbutton your top button and wear some bling—even fake chains and stones because no one here

An infamous incident took place in 1980 at the Mutiny Hotel when drugged-out hotel guests set off a fire alarm after lighting money in a hot tub, causing them to flee down a balcony awning when police arrived. (HistoryMiami Museum)

will question them. And comb your hair straight back so you look less like Cary Grant and more like a crooked politician."

We both laughed. "Just sit at the bar downstairs and see what's really going on because when I'm down there everyone acts like they're busy," he said.

Goldberg asked what my services cost. I quoted our standard bar-only rate of $100 plus reimbursement of covered expenses for a two-hour shopping visit, and if services involved being a room guest for a couple of nights, the cost would be commensurately more. He winced and looked away as if he'd bitten into a lemon.

"Are you shittin' me? How do you make any serious coin charging chump change? Hell, I make more money than that every night in my condom machines."

I explained that our mystery shopping business is often an entrée to other services we offer.

"Okay, fine, I'd rather be charged less than I expected than more," he said. "But I'm making this deal with you, *you,* meaning *you* are going to do the shoppings for me and not whatever asshole you send around. You get one membership card with your name on it and don't bring guests. No one else is to get your reports but me, and no one here is going to know why you're here, not even my security staff. Let's start off with a visit every two weeks, mixing up the days unless I call you with a specific day and time."

I agreed. This was too intriguing an assignment for one of my staffers anyway. We went over his bar modus operandi, such as register procedures, keeping tip containers separate from payments, and how bartenders should suggest refills when a glass becomes less than half filled rather than waiting for it to be empty or, worse yet, forcing a member to wave to get service.

We did a quick handshake and I figured that was that, but Goldberg wasn't through: "I don't want any written reports [about the Mutiny Club] in any of your files or computers. After you send them to me, I want your copy shredded or deleted on your end. Don't put any identifying information on your written reports to me, such as your company name or address."

He had more instructions. "When you call here," he continued, "ask to speak with Burt and use the name 'Fred Tucker' and I'll add that name to calls I'll accept. I don't want you sticking your nose into any other areas of the hotel—I've got cameras for that and my security guy fills me in on what's going on, most of which I'd rather not know. You got all that?"

I nodded. As I got up to leave, he again reached for my hand and this time he didn't let go right away. He looked me right in the eye without releasing his grip and said, "Doug, I consider a business relationship one of trust, especially when it comes to something as confidential as my internal security. Like in Vegas, what happens here, stays here. Don't fuck me and I won't fuck you."

I agreed, again wondering what I'd just gotten myself in to. I drove back to the office both intimidated and excited. That meeting with Goldberg began about six months of mystery shopping for his Mutiny Club. He mailed me a metallic membership card showing the club's pirate logo and imprinted with my first and last name. He asked that I review everything at the club from the moment of arrival to departing. That included door security, bouncers, bartenders, bar backs, table servers, entertainment, employee attitudes, bathroom cleanliness, VIP tables, how drunks were handled, etc. That's a typical range of observations at most clubs.

On my first shopping, a bartender—"You can call me Jose"—took my drink order of a Bacardi and diet cola with lime. After serving, he pointed at a nearby table and said, "You should'a been here an hour ago. Arnold Schwarzenegger was sitting right there."

I thought he might have been yanking me, but the fellow seated at my left overheard us and whipped out of his jacket pocket a napkin he claimed Schwarzenegger autographed for him. The movie *Terminator* that would propel Schwarzenegger to super stardom hadn't yet come out, but he was already well known as Mr. Universe and in movies like *Pumping Iron*.

I asked the starstruck fellow why Schwarzenegger departed and he said, "I dunno. He was probably getting asked to sign too many autographs."

Trying not to laugh or be sarcastic, I just nodded and looked away so as to end further chatter. Jose was less considerate of him. He glanced at me and shrugged, insinuating that you can't believe everything you hear from inebriated bar patrons.

My tack when working a bar counter for a client is initially just to soak up booze without getting drunk, look around as anyone would, and ask no suspicious questions. You don't stare at the cash register; you don't hit on women. I only order call or upper shelf brands, not well drinks (such as a Bacardi and cola and not a generic rum and cola, or a Chivas on the rocks rather than scotch on the rocks).

Tipping is crucial. A generous tipper increases the odds of being remembered more readily on future visits, even with multiple bartenders operating. Tips must be generous but not so high that there's no motivation for the bartender to pocket your drink payment. When drunks over-tip, bartenders attribute that to the liquor rather than the heart. I therefore tip $2 for a $7 drink. That certainly didn't make me a high roller in a setting where C-notes were commonly slipped to flirtatious table waitresses, but it didn't make me a typical one-buck piker either.

After my third visit, Jose greeted me. Although bartenders routinely pool tips, you'll still usually develop more rapport with the bartender who's most gregarious, which fortunately turned out to be Jose. During a down time, Jose moseyed over and began asking me questions, which is the perfect scenario: where I'm from, what do I do, tell me about your family.

Only on my fourth visit did I ask Jose about his background, after he again welcomed me. Anyone charging into a place asking questions, looking too intently at bar operations or obviously trying to cultivate sources will be spotted in a nanosecond by a veteran bartender and ID'ed as a shopper or, in the case of the Mutiny Club, an undercover ATF agent.

Jose, and through him the other bartenders, judged me a harmless club member, a guy with a voyeuristic tendency to stay on the sidelines and who got his jollies watching women and jet setters à la NYC's Club 54. It was cool seeing the occasional celebrity, as I've always been a movie and TV watcher, and the Mutiny Club was a celebrity magnet.

On various visits I observed Don Johnson and Philip Michael Thomas—co-stars of the then hit TV series *Miami Vice*. Others I saw come in and out included singer Rick James, who appeared to be higher than a kite, as well as Ted Kennedy looking buzzed. I approached Kennedy, figuring he'd likely not recall our tete-à-tete at a bar counter at The Breakers in Palm Beach about 13 years prior. I was right, he didn't remember me. Just as well, as I was in the Mutiny Club to do a shopping and not to get lost in a BS session.

Jose told me about recent visits of Paul Newman and Burt Reynolds. "The old man's [Goldberg's] Rolodex probably includes nearly everyone who shows up at the Academy Awards and walks the halls of the [U.S.] Capitol," he quipped.

I asked if any football players patronized the club. "Oh hell yeah," Jose replied. "Both from the Dolphins and Hurricanes." He didn't name any players and I knew better than to ask.

Most members and their guests sat in private reserved corrals with bottles of Dom Perignon or Möet jutting from ice buckets, the men sporting heavy gold chains, Rolexes with diamond bezels, oily ducktail and ponytail hairdos, and open shirts displaying forests of chest hair. At times I saw people openly doing toots at their table.

The place was a testosterone extravaganza, and painted ladies clung to their benefactors like white on rice, the entire entourage often disappearing "upstairs" in twos and threes and fours, assuredly to engage in all sorts of sexual and drug-inspired high jinks. As Goldberg had instructed, I stayed in the main bar and never visited the suites, hot tubs, or balconies.

Club staffers familiar with local law enforcement folks would signal their entry to employees with a finger gesture pointed at one of their eyes. At times the pungent aroma of marijuana wafted over the bar and no one complained or got arrested. The sexual energy was palpable, with all acts known to humans occurring within my sight. If an image of the word hedonism was to appear in a dictionary, the Mutiny Club would require no further definition.

I did observe occasional cases involving cash payments going into tip jars next to a register at the bar counter, waitresses swinging checks that had already been paid at least once before, under-pours of booze (often a telltale sign of an attempt to fool the liquor inventory), and keeping score, the latter at times performed with swizzle sticks or cherry stems dropped into a cocktail glass to assess the overage a bartender can skim when closing out.

None of those perpetrators involved Jose and those who did appear in my reports were summarily fired. I also included in reports observations of employees being lax or displaying indifferent behavior as well as excellent performances. I always recommended to clients that they handle minor infractions by confronting those guilty and to deliver constructive criticism to obtain improved performances; for those going above and beyond duty, give them attaboys or attagirls. But that didn't resonate with Goldberg. Ongoing visits made it clear that those reported as acting a bit below par would also be gone.

I always recognized that our shoppers wielded a sharp double-edged sword that necessitated absolute objectivity when dealing with people's livelihoods, but Goldberg wouldn't tolerate even the tiniest transgression. On one occasion when providing an oral report to Goldberg following a shopping visit, I brought the issue of positive motivation up to him and not to expect perfect performances 100 percent of the time.

His response: "Fuck 'em, we've got a list a mile long of people who want to work here."

As such, I purposely left out such minor things as briefly leaning against a wall as a breather or accidentally spilling a drink or a stall in the men's room low on paper. I know that's not de rigueur in providing a comprehensive report, but Goldberg's tyrannical behavior crossed the line and in my opinion was unfair.

One evening while at Mutiny's bar counter I saw a scary-looking man at a nearby table. His eyes were dark, menacing, like a shark. I asked one of the bartenders who he was.

"I don't know his name, but I'm pretty sure he's some sort of wise guy," he replied. I later found out his identity: Aniello "Neil" Dellacroce, the Gambino underboss. Two burly guys sat with him, the type of fellows you'd rather not cross.

"Wow, would it be cool if I said hello and sent him a drink?"

"Yeah, if you want to get your ass kicked," he said resolutely. "Those guys won't let anyone near him unless he [Dellacroce] gives the nod."

The same bartender later leaned in and whispered, "Hey listen, you name damn near any Mafia guy still walking around and they've been here at one time or another. One thing I've learned, unless a mob guy starts a conversation with you, don't mess with them—I've seen members roughed up for overstepping their boundaries with people they don't know."

I glanced over at Dellacroce, studying him. At one point we made eye contact and he glared at me until I looked away. It literally sent a shiver down my spine. If there's a stereotype of the menacing-looking Mafioso, he's at the top of my list.

Besides occasional feedback from Jose, during one of my visits about three months into the Mutiny shoppings, he introduced me to a bar waitress calling herself Sapphire. I learned that many of the employees involved in guest interaction used a pseudonym for personal safety reasons, especially the females. I'd noticed her from previous visits and reported on her congeniality with members and energetic work ethic. It wasn't as busy as usual, being a Tuesday afternoon, and she invited me to sit with her at an open table. At first I wondered if Jose was pimping and setting me up with her.

We made small talk and I blurted out that I'm married. Sapphire laughed. She wasn't as attractive as some of the other waitresses but was alluring in her own right, with shiny brown hair, pretty blue eyes, and a killer figure. I judged her to be in her mid-20s.

"Honey, if only single guys came in here for drinks it would be a lonely place," she said with a grin. "The married guys are usually hornier than the single ones. Don't worry, I'm not going to jump you."

I perceived an opportunity to learn more about the Mutiny Club than just from Jose and my observations. We chatted amiably about her hometown of New Orleans, her degree in psychology (the same as mine) and how exciting life was for her in Miami. When more guests started flowing in she said she had to get to work, but added, "Hey, I like you. We'll chat some more sometime if you're around."

After two more friendly chats with Sapphire in ensuing visits, I found out she was fond of fishing. Clearing it first with Goldberg ("Yeah, see what she's got to say, but don't fuck her.") I invited her to an outing in my boat with Mrs. Kelly aboard and she could invite a couple of friends to come along. She agreed to do so on her next day off and we made the arrangements to meet at Matheson Hammock Park.

She arrived with two female friends not employed at the club; my wife didn't want to go. We fished several locations in Biscayne Bay until making a visit to Elliott Key. The three ladies disappeared down a trail, returning in about 15 minutes obviously stoned. But getting Sapphire to chat away from the Mutiny Club offered a treasure trove of behind-the-scenes gossip.

Sapphire disclosed that she sometimes received huge tips and "entertained" some of the members and guests. "If you don't, you'll be let go," she said. Sapphire spoke of gunshots being fired by inebriated bodyguards and that she even heard of a murder that took place on the premises that was covered up.

She added, "It can be dangerous, especially around people who are on drugs or booze. A lot of people hide weapons on them and the bouncers at times have their hands full."

Sapphire described Goldberg as a merciless tyrant who would fire people "left and right" for the most trivial reasons. "He terminated one girl because a member complained to him that she wouldn't give him a blow job," she exclaimed, shaking her head. "A girl can make more than a $100,000 a year there, but you can't ever complain about what you see and 'put out' to important members. And yes, I know what that makes me."

She heard from others at the club that the best way to deal with "Mr. Goldberg" when he'd be high strung was to bring up his art collection or alternative medicine, but for the most part, she stayed clear of him.

"So much for being a nice Catholic girl," she laughed. "Like with most

The Mutiny Hotel has gone through several renovations since Goldberg sold it in 1984 and it's now an elegant and respectable establishment. (Michael D. Kelly)

employees, the money is too good to pass up. I intend to work there another couple of years. But if you have moral issues, it's not the place to be."

I reported to Goldberg the essence of my day with Sapphire and revealed nothing to get her in trouble—after all, her job performance at the Mutiny was outstanding. Unfortunately for Sapphire's desire to hang on for another two years and for that matter Jose and all the others on the payroll of the Mutiny Club, she would not be employed much longer.

In January 1984, Goldberg sold the property for a reported $17.5 million. Months before that, I had to end the mystery shopping service there or, as one might say, he fired me. Goldberg liked my reporting feedback and it evidently helped him tighten up his operation a bit, but then he made a demand that went too far: He insisted that I spy on other clubs for him.

Perhaps he was considering buying another club somewhere. Who knows? But my firm policy was that our reports went only to the owner of that business, and I refused to spy on competitors. To do otherwise, I told him, would risk my state PI license being revoked and went against what remnants of a conscience I still had. He persisted but I wouldn't budge.

"Fuck you then," he said. "You've done your last shopping for me."

Just as well. I'd had my fill to the point that I began to dread the visits to that den of sin and debauchery, particularly after learning from Sapphire about shootings that took place—I damn sure didn't want to catch a stray bullet.

After all my visits to the Mutiny Club, I managed to not get high (other than inhaling second-hand ganja) or to get laid despite the constant temptations there. It was the most prodigious pickup bar I've ever seen. But I can only wonder if Goldberg skimmed on top of the millions he most certainly pocketed legally. Even being a tyrant, I'm sure he had a human side that finally tired after 16 years of running the most boisterous and infamous club in Miami's history.

Equally a mystery to me is how downright remarkable it is that Burton Goldberg managed to stay in business despite undercover surveillance of the club by government agents and constant threats from authorities to put a lock on the door. It would be jumping to conclusions to state that palms were greased and heads were turned to keep it all going. The property later reopened as a sanitized version of its former self, but that incarnation never caught on, and it closed in 1986. Another version in the form of luxury condominiums opened in 1999, and the Mutiny Hotel is a legitimate establishment and still at the venerable location of 2951 South Bayshore Drive.

Burton Goldberg's Mutiny Club at Sailboat Bay. There will never be another quite like it. I hope not.

10

NOT-SO-BLUE EYES

Recalling the work I'd done for Frank Sinatra, I'm quite certain that a mysterious person contacting me likely came by his referral, but it's still a mystery. Here's what happened: One day I received a call at my office from a Mr. DeMarco. Speaking so softly I could barely hear him, he wanted to set up a meeting, but not just any ol' across-the-table meeting.

"I understand you're a golfer," he said with a voice so husky it could pull a dog sled. "You want to play a round at Biltmore? Playing golf or poker with someone always reveals a person's true nature."

Biltmore Golf Course is a venerable hotel and 18-hole layout in Coral Gables. Built in 1925 with an historic history when it comes to legendary players competing in tournaments of yesteryear, its use extended in World War II to serving as a veteran's hospital. It was also the home course of the University of Miami's golf team when I attended.

Not feeling particularly comfortable at the prospect of spending four or five hours playing golf with someone I'd never met, I suggested lunch instead. Due to the high-privacy and sensitivity regarding contract security services, it was not unusual to talk with someone away from their place of business or home to discuss my services, but no one ever suggested doing so while engaging in a sporting activity.

Mr. DeMarco agreed and suggested on the upcoming Saturday we get together at "Bobby Rubino's—A Place for Ribs" in southwest Miami. Did he somehow know that I lived just a few minutes from there on Kendall Drive? Maybe not, but I did later learn that that rib chain was reputedly mob owned.

When we met, he appeared to be in his 70s but quite dapper and lucid despite the thick-lensed glasses. Rather than some sort of tough guy, he resembled an amiable uncle type with a long face, big nose and receding hairline. He somehow knew what I looked like as he stood at a table for two in the rear of the restaurant.

"Are you Mr. DeMarco?" I asked as our hands clasped.

"Let me introduce myself," he replied with a genuine smile. "Yes, I'm Mr. DeMarco, but just call me Jimmy." That of course confirmed my suspicious of his using an alias.

After we studied the menu and ordered, he got right to the point. "You have a service we might be interested in. Fill me in a little on how you find bugs and the equipment you use."

I did so, outlining the electronic and physical search phases of a proper sweep. He leaned forward, intrigued by it all. I showed him a picture of some of my gear that included a spectrum analyzer, carrier current detector, phone testing equipment as well as other techy gadgets of varying use and capability.

He wanted to know how each piece worked. I began to suspect that maybe he was looking to get into the technical surveillance countermeasures business as a competitor.

"Geez, all that stuff musta cost a pretty penny," he went on. "Tell me about your training and experience."

I did so briefly, still unnerved about the grilling, but he portrayed a disarming manner. His next request was expected.

"Name some of your clients."

I told him that's a no-no due to the high confidentiality involved. "I never give out the names of my clients."

He studied me a moment. When someone does that, I look them right back in the eyes and say nothing. He spoke first.

"Good, that's the answer I wanted. You obviously know your craft and come recommended by someone I trust," he said, lowering his voice.

"I represent a wealthy family with offices and business locations around the nation. What would you say if we offered you an annual contract that either party can end at any time—no commitments either way—if you'll give us a week of your time each month and we pay you $200,000 per year—in cash, if you prefer."

That was a lot to process. Taken aback for a moment I finally inquired about the identity of his "family." I later found out it's a wealthy family alright, as in the Genovese family, but he could tell I was stunned and noncommittal at that time.

"We need confidentiality too," he quickly stated. "I'll be more forthcoming about that if we get to the next stage. Let's take things one step at a time—don't give me an answer now. Think over my proposal and I'll check back with you in a few days. If you're up to exploring this more, I'll tell you more. If not, no harm done."

The congenial mobster Vincent "Jimmy Blue Eyes" Alo frolicking in his younger years. (Carole and Kevin Russo)

It amazed me how slowly he ate lunch. I'm not a fast eater but was done when Jimmy still had more than half a plateful. An ice chewer, I sipped a tea and the teeth gnashing didn't seem to faze him. We didn't talk while he slowly chomped away, but I didn't feel uncomfortable. When he finished the check arrived and Jimmy grabbed it. I said if there's a next time, it's on me. He grinned.

As nice a gentleman as I've ever met.

That evening I talked to my wife about the conversation and the offer. We agreed that $200,000 would be mighty nice, but our instincts matched in that it sounded too good to be true. Where's the catch? Is Mr. DeMarco or Jimmy really a government agent trying to see if I'll agree to doing something illegal such as plant bugs in the U.S. without a court order? Is he a front man for a drug cartel? Or is he in fact representing a wealthy family like the Rockefellers or Du Ponts? Perhaps a Mafioso?

I was already making a good living with a couple of Cadillacs in the driveway of a large corner home in a tony suburb of Kendall, but wasn't knocking down enough money to scoff at 200 grand. I checked around if anyone knew a Jimmy DeMarco, but came up with goose eggs. Then again, my research sources only entailed phone calls to a few law enforcement people willing to share intel as well as a brother-in-law who was a major in the Dade County Public Safety Department (now the Miami-Dade Police Department). It would be a few years from then before online research and firms offering background checks made looking up someone easy, but not back then. Many offices like mine still depended on IBM typewriters.

With the paternal desire of wanting to be around as my two small children grew up, I fell on the side of playing it safe. When Jimmy called three days later, I expressed my hesitation. The offer is tempting, I said, but I can't agree to work for any client on an annual contract without even knowing for sure who it is. Jimmy replied that that's not something he could discuss over the phone, and asked if we could meet again per his reprised offer to play a round of golf at Biltmore.

I appreciated his desire to not speak over the phone, and though I found it strange that again he insisted we play golf, I agreed. I also wanted to know who referred me. I'd guessed it to be Al Malnik. When I arrived at Biltmore with my clubs, Jimmy had already paid my greens fee and our cart. It surprised me that as a two-some the starter didn't pair us with others as customary, but being on a Tuesday and not crowded it didn't surprise me too much.

The author didn't realize when first meeting Jimmy Blue Eyes and playing a round of golf together that he was a highly respected caporegime in the Genovese family. (Carole and Kevin Russo)

I could immediately tell that Jimmy was an experienced player in both his natty attire and decent golf game. As we rode along in the cart and chatted during the afternoon, Jimmy said he knew that I'd played on the University of Miami golf team years before and that he was a friend of Jimmy Burns, the former sports editor of the *Miami Herald* and avid golfer. My golf scholarship to UM was so named in Burns's honor and paid for by the newspaper.

After the round of golf, we did a 19th hole chat in the clubhouse lounge. I liked Jimmy. He was charming and chatty, asking me questions about how I took up golf, my major in college, how I got into the security biz and other small talk. I felt it only fair for me to delve into who he was and how he contacted me.

First off, I asked if Al Malnik had referred me to him. He acted like he was gut shot.

"Absolutely not," he replied with disgust, his face contorted. Jimmy said he was referred by "an attorney of mine" but didn't identify him or her. And I still didn't know his real name, so I asked about it.

He laughed. "You couldn't find anything about a Jimmy DeMarco, eh? Well, I'd rather I tell you than finding out from someone else eventually," he said. "I'm not what I'd call famous but I am known around town and in many places. My name is Vincent Alo. Some call me Jimmy Blue Eyes."

He smirked when I mentioned the irony that his name isn't Jimmy and he didn't have blue eyes.

"I know. It's a nickname that stuck," he said.

Only recently did I learn the real story about the blue eyes label from Kevin Russo, whose mom Carole was Alo's niece. Both Carole and Kevin were very close to Alo and still speak highly of him.

"He got the nickname Jimmy Blue Eyes as a teenager from a female cousin," said Kevin. "They were dancing together to a popular song back then called 'Brown Eyes, Why So Blue?' That's how she got the idea for the nickname."

As to where the name Jimmy came from, Russo said, "At one time 'Jimmy' was the Italian-American nickname for Vincent." Whatever the derivation, I knew that Mafiosi had monikers such as Capone's "Scarface," Scarpa's "The Grim Reaper," Anastasia's "The Lord High Executioner," Persico's "The Snake" and so on.

But back to my chat with Jimmy. I asked if he was a member of organized crime?

That produced a scoff and a head shake. "You know Doug, that terminology is vague and turns me off. But I know what you're getting at. I grew up in the Bronx long ago and as a kid became friends with other Italian guys. We suffered greatly from prejudice just like your ancestors being Irish did in those days. We were at the bottom rung of getting jobs in New York City, and even if we got hired, we'd get paid less than others.

"Some of us worked for others as I did for a while and never got anywhere," he continued, "so we pooled our talents and made money ourselves. A lot of money. I don't have any regrets. Follow me around and you'll see the respect I get."

I nodded and admitted my fascination with the Mafia, that I'd heard through the grapevine from security and law enforcement friends and read in the papers about Mafia families in most major cities and in particular New York City.

"I realize you're on the fringes of that with the work you do," he said. "Sure, I hobnobbed with Luciano and Lansky and Costello and many others. You'll find my name in all sorts of reports and stories about *Cosa Nostra*. I miss the action and excitement of the casino business. Even so, I don't seek publicity and try to stay off radar screens even though all those in the life and joints I visit know me.

"Your curiosity is understood," he went on, "and what you do intrigues me as well because wiretaps and bugs have been the main weapons in confronting many of my business associates. But please don't ask me if I ever did this or ever did that. That's like me asking you if you're ever cheated on your taxes. You're not going to say, 'Yes, please report me to the IRS so they can start an investigation.' I'm amazed at how often reporters ask me to rat out myself and others, and even the FBI and prosecutors do it. When I *have* tried to answer questions truthfully and cooperate it's come back to bite me in the ass."

I reached for the check and once again he beat me to it. "No, I always pay."

I agreed but told him to let me at least look at it. I juggled the check in my hands and dropped it on the table. "There, I handled it."

That amused him big time. But I was still curious about two things: If he'd retired from the life, why ask me about doing 'work' for his business associates? And why did he approach me instead of someone less credentialed in the Mafia?

As if reading my mind, he remarked, "I never said I was retired and never said I wasn't, but at my age I've slowed up and mostly let others carry the ball now," he said. "But I know what's going on. I made the approach to you because of my attorney's reference and finding out about your Jimmy Burns scholarship—my passion is golf."

Hoping to dig into some details about his life, I found he seemed to again anticipate my curiosity and cut me off.

"Look, I've told you all I'm going to say about me. You seem like a decent fellow and I enjoyed our round of golf, and maybe we'll talk more about our lives if you agree to help my pals. I don't talk about my past much and to be honest if you decide to go forward, I wouldn't be your contact, but maybe we can tee it up now and then—you're a good golfer and I try harder and enjoy it more when playing with talented players."

Our 18 holes together were genial. One would never suspect Jimmy's prominence in the Mafia without knowing his history because of his easygoing manner and likability. We didn't mark a scorecard that day even though I outplayed him. But I surmised that in his earlier days he probably could have given me a challenge. He'd remarked about how most of his former golfing pals had either passed away or were too old now to swing a club.

Would Jimmy Blue Eyes become a golfing partner going forward, I wondered?

That was not to be. Before departing, he took a deep sigh and asked if I was "in or out" on the proposal. I told Jimmy it would be too dangerous for me, and without changing expression he asked why.

I told him about how some elements in the government can double-cross you.

He cocked his head, nodded and said, "Yeah, I get you. It's true, you can't always trust the government. But it's taking risks that separates the winners from the also rans, Doug. Life is a crap shoot and a horse race—you will often lose, but the winning times far outweigh them."

I responded that perhaps years ago when I didn't have a young family I'd roll the dice, but not now. I added that the last time I bit on the "working for a wealthy family" scenario it ended with me embroiled in Watergate.

"Yeah, I know about that too," he said with a knowing smile. "I read your testimony—I'm sort of a Watergate historian." He was referring to the Senate Watergate Committee hearings before which I testified in October 1973. [NOTE: Read the full story in my memoir *Dirty Trickster, Corporate Spy*.]

We shook hands, I left the Biltmore, and that was the last I ever heard from Jimmy Blue Eyes. Since then, with the advent of books about the Mafia, endless TV documentaries, the glamorization of the mobster movies and now ex-wise guys with YouTube channels, I've learned plenty about just how powerful and influential Vincent Alo was. A capo in the Genovese family and best friends and business partners with numerous mobsters—particularly Luciano and Lansky in the bootlegging era and before and after helping to form a crime syndicate in the early 1930s—his life stretched across almost the entirety of the twentieth century. He and wife Flo were married for 60 years, a testament to their loyalty and love.

He lived that life in New York City and in South Florida, overseeing with his lifelong buddy Lansky and others the burgeoning casino biz in New York, Las Vegas, pre-1950 South Florida and in Cuba until Castro's takeover. Suffering from dementia many years later, he died on March 9, 2001, at age 96.

When reading about him or viewing the imposing hotel tower of Biltmore Golf Course in Coral Gables, I reminisce about the fortuitous opportunity of spending time with Jimmy Blue Eyes. For a more personal tome on Jimmy, a great read is *Me and Jimmy Blue Eyes* written by his niece Carole Russo.

11

~~~~~~

MORE MIAMI MAFIOSI

The number of bad guys depending on ill-gotten gains who migrated to Florida started like a slow drip in the 1930s until the end of Prohibition. Big names like Lanksy and Capone had already discovered the comforts and comparative innocence of Florida as part-time residents. Most still needed to tend to "family business" up north, but some tired of commuting and handled mob affairs via lower-level messengers. And who's to blame them when choosing between listening to the splatter of hail on your windshield or hearing the gentle sound of bamboo windchimes on your patio?

Coinciding with the "discovery" of Florida was the loss of bootlegging income after 1933, which as we know the Mafia already anticipated. Another spigot of cash would be needed aside from the usual racketeering activities, and that meant focusing on gambling. Post-Prohibition, underground speakeasies that had offered card and dice games no longer required access with a password through a peephole, and most of those joints were small in size, so as to be less conspicuous to cops during those furious 13 years with no legal booze. Larger floor spaces would allow more elbow room and greater critical mass, and that entailed expanding existing footage, such as converting hotel conference rooms or building stand-alone casinos from scratch.

As casino gambling surged in Florida—particularly in South Florida—the scent of money and easily corruptible cops drew mobsters to the Sunshine State by the hundreds and soon thousands. Aside from gambling income, associated criminal activities snowballed and became controlled by the same kingpins, such as bolita, bookmaking, loan sharking, prostitution and eventually illegal drugs.

We've already covered some interesting characters. In this chapter I present vignettes on other prominent Mafiosi who moved to South Florida to represent their family's interests or to start trouble on their own.

Mike "Trigger Mike" Coppola began a life of crime in NYC with Lucky Luciano's gang and quickly earned a reputation for violence both as a gangster and in his personal life. (Button Guys of The New York Mafia)

Mike "Trigger Mike" Coppola

Coppola discovered the wonders of Miami Beach in the early 1940s. He owned a home near the exclusive La Gorce Country Club, where decades later Arnold Palmer became the club's touring pro. In 1950 Coppola bought a residence at 4431 Alton Road, a major north–south inland route on Miami Beach.

He remained a major factor in organized crime in Florida until the 1960s. Few mobsters networked more than Coppola when it came to diversifying his criminal activities. He became tight with Lucky Luciano and enjoyed a 40-year friendship with Meyer Lansky, who as we know became established early on in South Florida and was capable of opening many doors for his business partners.

Coppola was a short, lumpy sort of guy who physically and mentally abused both his wives. Doris Lehman, his dark-haired and pretty first wife beginning in 1943, was likely murdered to prevent her from testifying against him. She got killed in a hospital bed a day after giving birth to a girl, the couple's second child. Coppola quickly had his deceased wife cremated to avoid an autopsy.

His second wife, Ann Draumann—also attractive and about the same height as the unsightly Coppola—had a prior mob connection through her first marriage. When she was introduced to Coppola, he instantly became smitten, wining and dining her with considerable gusto. She evidently overlooked his appearance and favored another tenure as the wife of a gangster.

Married to Coppola for only five years beginning in 1955, Ann endured constant abuse and once even dodged a bullet fired by her psychopathic husband. She almost suffered the same fate as Doris, barely escaping with her life after getting beaten by two thugs her husband hired because she agreed to testify against him for tax fraud. She had already suffered the indignity of a series of abortions while living with Coppola in Miami Beach—the first just a few months after they married—due to her sadistic husband's purposeful refusal to use a condom.

Ann also accused Coppola of giving her daughter Joan drugs and sexually assaulting her. They divorced in 1960, and Ann and daughter crossed the Atlantic on a ship for a new life. When she settled in Rome, she mailed damning letters about Coppola's criminal activities to the IRS and U.S. Attorney General Bobby Kennedy.

His treatment of wives alone provides a dark window into a wretched persona that paralleled his reputation as a ruthless murderer with no conscience. He became a member of Luciano's crime family in NYC, taking over for him when Lucky became unlucky and ended up in prison in 1936. Coppola soon thereafter became underboss when Vito Genovese went on the lam to dodge a murder charge.

Coppola controlled several unions and got rich in the cigarette vending machine business as he rose to the rank of capo in the Genovese family. It's said that Coppola's crew was the largest and most feared of all NYC families. For a time, Patsy Erra served as a hit man and Coppola's driver. They would later reunite when both resided in Miami Beach at the height of their prominence in South Florida crime circles.

Coppola became the Genovese family's point man in Florida with his hand in many different criminal enterprises. He co-owned a casino called Club Collins on Miami Beach and backed big-time bookmakers, the latter resulting in investigations that banned Coppola from Tropical Park and other horseracing tracks.

Coppola also operated a casino out of the Midtown Social Club. Wielding his money and contacts, he became a board member of General Development Corporation, which grew to be Florida's largest real estate firm. GDC served as the conduit to buy potential casino sites in Florida as well as the Bahamas—in particular, Grand Bahama Island.

In 1954 when the Fontainebleau Hotel opened, Coppola turned one of the poolside cabanas into his criminal headquarters. He had so much money flowing in from interests in Nevada, Cuba, and the Bahamas casinos with partners Meyer Lansky and Vincent Alo that his wife Ann later claimed he stashed hundreds of thousands of dollars about their Miami Beach abode. And that cash didn't even count the proceeds from loan sharking and other illegal enterprises.

Like many gangsters, along the way Coppola got pinched and imprisoned as law enforcement tried to stem the nonstop criminal activities of the Mafia. In 1941 Coppola was hit with charges for crimes that included murder, burglary and drug trafficking. However, he would avoid the long arm of the law for another 20 years despite his name appearing in numerous investigations. The first blow didn't involve prison but did put a serious dent in his pocket when he became blacklisted in all Nevada casinos in 1960. A year later Coppola received indictments for not paying hundreds of thousands in back taxes—a result based mainly on former wife Ann's testimony.

Coppola served only nine months of a four-year sentence for the tax evasion in Atlanta's penitentiary, where coincidentally another inmate turned out to be Vito Genovese, still in the slammer for drug trafficking. Another guy wearing prison duds with Coppola during his brief incarceration was Joe Valachi, who would soon cooperate with the feds and in public testimony in 1963 reveal insider details about the workings and personalities in the Mafia that shocked the world.

By the time Coppola was released, others had taken over his various operations because the mob bosses decided they'd had enough of the adverse publicity resulting from his horrid personal life. Coppola, ordered to retire and to keep his mouth shut if he wanted to live, spent his final years traveling to various countries when not idly following his shadow around the house in Miami Beach. He died of kidney failure in 1966 at the age of 66 while being treated in a Boston hospital.

Alfred "Freddy" George Felice

The Philadelphia mob needed to follow suit like the other families and establish a Florida connection, particularly in Miami. That major connection came to them by way of Freddy Felice during the time Angelo Bruno emerged as Philly's boss. It's nearly impossible to separate Felice's involvement in Florida without including Bruno as well as John Simone.

Freddy Felice served as a well-connected Mafioso and the Philly mob's point man in Florida. (Button Guys of The New York Mafia)

The interrelationships of those three men, not only in Florida but in NYC, New Jersey, and Pennsylvania, are numerous, although in this book we're focused on Florida.

As was so often the case with Mafiosi who ended up in Florida, Felice, born in 1912, grew up in the Bronx and East Harlem in NYC with affiliations to made men in the Lucchese and Genovese families. As such, he was already on the *Cosa Nostra* organizational charts known by law enforcement entities. He went by several aliases, including Freddy Franco and Freddy Red Shirt in homage to his brother Peter (a.k.a. Petey Red Shirt), who got made into the Gambino family before being murdered on New Year's Eve in 1936.

Freddy Felice became tight in his NYC neighborhood with Patsy Erra and Mike Coppola, and later renewed their friendships when all three owned homes in Miami. In 1931 in NYC, Felice got pinched for vagrancy, a favorite charge at the time by cops who loathed Italians, Irishmen, Jews and other nationalities they considered lower class.

In 1935 Freddy partnered in a racketeering scheme—the exact activity isn't clear but was probably shylocking—in Long Island with Joseph "Pip the Blind" Gagliano, a Lucchese member, resulting in their arrests along with Ida, Felice's wife, and Gagliano's sister. That same year Felice again got pinched, this time for the suspected murder of Harold "Shake" Brooks, but he beat the rap.

Up until the mid-1940s Felice mainly trafficked heroin, after which he moved to Miami Beach. His reputation within law enforcement went with him, however, and in 1948 the cops got him off the streets briefly by arresting him for vagrancy. Felice's name frequently appeared on the police blotters in South Florida, including for a jewel heist in 1953.

Although a Florida resident, Felice kept in close touch with former mob associates via frequent visits to New York City and Philadelphia. His numerous Mafia connections and drug trafficking activities undoubtedly led him to become a friend of Santo Trafficante Jr., who had taken over from his father the Mafia family by the same name based in Tampa. Felice and Trafficante Jr. co-owned a pest control company in Miami used as a money laundering vehicle with Angelo Bruno and Agostino Amato, the latter a member of the Gambino family.

His relationship with Bruno is often framed as difficult, perhaps stemming from Bruno being displeased for some reason with Felice's handling of a newsstand and vending business owned by Bruno. The newsstand, located at the King Cole Apartments off the Intracoastal Waterway, was meant to be a front for bookmaking and money laundering.

Felice also took charge of local labor unions, although Florida was, and still is, a right-to-work state whereby employees aren't forced to join a union. That rendered the unions far less powerful than those up north.

A faulty ticker dogged Felice in his later years, including heart attacks that often required hospitalization. He died in January 1979 of "natural causes," most likely heart failure.

John Simone

Philly don Angelo Bruno was fatally blasted with a shotgun in 1980 because Mafia bosses in NYC families considered him too nice a guy and therefore permissive of encroachments by unaffiliated drug dealers into their territories. Bruno had gained control of the Philly mob in 1959 and developed trusted ties to subordinates such as Freddy Felice and John Simone.

Simone's death has been in the spotlight more than his life of crime, as mentioned earlier in the book. It's worth adding some details to that. In 1980 Gambino boss Paul Castellano ordered hit man Salvatore "Sammy the Bull" Gravano's crew to take out Simone. That they did so has previously been touched upon, but not before kidnapping Simone from a New Jersey country club and driving in a van to Staten Island on the premise Gravano would help Simone take over the Philly mob.

Gravano spent hours in the van chatting amiably with Simone while awaiting the green light from the Commission to assassinate Simone.

Gravano—who had never met Simone—developed a kinship with the 69-year-old mobster due to a mutual respect of *Cosa Nostra* and its traditions of respect and *omerta*. Simone, realizing he'd been duped and was probably facing murder, suffered a heart attack soon after being abducted. At Simone's request, Gravano administered his medication (likely a nitroglycerin tablet) to keep him alive.

Simone wanted to die with "honor" by being shot by a made man rather than from a natural cause. Simone went along with his own murder willingly and without resistance. Trapped as a captive by Gravano's crew, he really had no choice as they both knew Gravano could not countermand a hit order.

Turning back the clock, Simone was made a capo in Bruno's family in 1959. He took part in various racketeering activities in Philly and Trenton, New Jersey. Some records reflect Simone visiting Florida as early as 1940 and residing in West Palm Beach.

In 1948 Simone moved to South Florida and made his home in Miami's North Bay Village. His residence was a 5-iron shot from Dean Martin's restaurant on what was then known as the 79th Street Causeway, one of several roadways between Miami and Miami Beach. Considering that Florida was considered an "open state" by the Mafia in comparison to the growing law enforcement presence elsewhere, mobsters could meet and cavort openly such as Dean Martin's place while experiencing less heat. It's been reported that through his friendship with Dean Martin, Simone and other Mafiosi cavorted with Rat Packers like Sinatra and Sammy Davis Jr. whenever they visited Miami Beach, all under the watchful eye of the FBI.

As 1980 came to an end, the power of the Philadelphia family in South Florida waned after the deaths of Simone, Felice and Bruno. However, Nicky Scarfo—the successor to Bruno as Philly boss—lived in Fort Lauderdale before being given a life sentence (he died in prison) and Joey Merlino (a main player in the upcoming chapter on the Palm Beaches) moved to Boca Raton and, besides stints in prison, as of this writing still allegedly has influence with the Philly family.

Hundreds of other Mafia members and drug kingpins residing all or part-time in South Florida could deservedly receive subheads of their own: Vincent Teriaca, Ettore Zappi, Jimmy Fratianno, Joe Battle Sr. and Jr., Griselda Blanco, Abraham Rydz, Domenico Pollina, Anthony Russo, Charles Castello, and John Tronoline. Perhaps a book sequel will include them.

12

CUBAN CONTROL

"If I were you, I wouldn't include anything in your book about the Cuban Mafia in Miami," advised longtime friend and Miamian Al Pflueger Jr.

"Why?"

"Because it might not be conducive to your health," he replied. "They control everything here [in Miami] and they don't like people who talk about who they are and what they do."

Point well taken, Al. However, two things I'll point out: I could not faithfully compile a book about organized crime in Florida and *not* mention the Cuban Mafia, and I'm *not* going to mention names or specifics that would subject anyone to legal jeopardy.

That said, this chapter presents the basis for how the Cuban Mafia in Miami began and how it grew into an organization with power and influence. In addition, I lived in Miami for over 20 years, went to the University of Miami, owned a very successful security firm in South Florida and formed deep relationships with Cubans of all ages, with many continuing to this day.

A smattering of Cubans inhabited Miami and other Florida towns and cities since the 1800s. The history of significant Cuban influence in Miami escalated when Castro toppled Batista in 1959. That provoked thousands of disaffected former supporters of the bearded dictator to flee the island. They'd been duped and betrayed; they didn't buy into communism and the promises of societal prosperity. And time would prove they were right.

Leapfrogging across the Gulf Stream from northern environs of Cuba to Miami became frequent. Boats began arriving with men, women and children of all ages; some started families or added to families.

The failed Bay of Pigs invasion in 1962 consisting of militant Cubans trained in Everglades camps by the CIA didn't quell the hope of retaking their island. Instead, it swelled the ranks of anti-Castro paramilitary exile organizations in Miami (Alpha 66, Brigade 2506, etc.) with endless invasion and assassination plans that ultimately fizzled. Most Cubans simply wanted to restart their lives and secured domiciles or took up residence with predecessors already ensconced among suburbs of Hialeah and Calle Ocho (S.W. Eighth Street), which quickly expanded east, west, north and south. By the late 1970s, Spanish could be heard every day in every corner of Miami north of Homestead.

I witnessed all that Latin growth as a high school and college student in Miami. Both of my children were born in Miami's Baptist Hospital near our home in Kendall. My security business was based in Hialeah just off the Palmetto Expressway. It became a necessity for companies to hire bilingual secretaries. Cuban staff members became company officers and many started ventures of their own. I formed tight friendships with Cuban Americans in college, some of whom still remain in touch—with rare exceptions, once a Cuban becomes your friend, it's an eternal bond of loyalty.

Cubans soaked up most of the job market, angering many in Miami's black and brown population. In fact, the entire black community felt left out and threatened to stage boycotts to impact the tourism industry, which quickly resulted in Miami-Dade County and the City of Miami taking steps to ensure more inclusion of its black citizens. That helped, but violent Haitian gangs still objected and made their presence known even though their numbers didn't match those of Cuban organizations.

Want ads in the *Miami Herald* began specifying "bilingual preferred," meaning non-Spanish-speaking applicants were often left out in the cold. Non-Latins were at times passed over for Cubans when promotions came up in order to recognize the ever-expanding Cuban population in Miami.

An example that hit home involved my then brother-in-law, Dave Watson. A major and district commander for the Dade County Public Safety Department (now the Miami-Dade Police Department) with nearly 30 years of service, Watson told me he lost out on a promotion to a Cuban officer with lesser credentials. True or not, that wasn't an uncommon gripe among white managers in the public and private sectors of Miami. Soon thereafter Watson threw in the towel and got out of town, taking his pension with him to Colorado. More than a few other like-minded gringos ceded Miami to the Cubans and moved away.

As the Cuban population expanded and became a majority block, so did its political clout. Dade County managers such as Ray Goode throughout most of the 1970s and Merrett Stierheim through the mid-1980s soon gave way to Latino managers. The same happened with Miami mayors and councilmembers. Cuban Americans snapped up state legislature and U.S. congressional seats.

The influx of Cubans has enriched Miami with its Latin culture, but Miami also alleg-edly serves as a base for the powerful Cuban Mafia. (floridamemory.com)

Radio and TV stations that up until the 1970s had almost exclusively featured American-born (i.e., white non-Cuban) hosts gradually integrat-ed on-air talent who could speak Spanish to appeal better to their listeners and viewers. Even though almost all Cuban Americans could speak Eng-lish, they related more to those who spoke their native tongue. Nowadays, if you tune through the radio or TV stations in Miami you'll encounter few white Anglo-Saxon American hosts. Political observers immediately rec-ognized the reality that Miami had become de facto a Cuban city, and from a purely democratic aspect that's the way it should be. The majority rules.

While this isn't a detailed history of Miami's social and political evolu-tion, an elementary understanding of it is required to bridge the emer-gence of the Cuban Mafia. As the population of honest and industrious Cuban Americans multiplied, so did the criminal-minded among them. The Mariel boatlifts beginning in 1980 involved thousands of Cubans escaping communism on makeshift sailboats and rafts to risk 90+ miles adrift in Gulf Stream waters between the northwestern Cuban port city of Mariel and the 110-mile stretch of islands that form the Florida Keys.

A friend named Dan Baker lived in Marathon in the Keys, and as a pilot and videographer made a tidy sum selling to Miami TV stations and national news outlets aerial footage of desperate and brave Cuban refugees floating in the Gulf Stream. For months on a daily basis, fishermen, charter boat captains, the Coast Guard and even cruise ships rescued near-drowning escapees on rafts of utterly shabby construction. Many didn't survive, drowning en route in high seas, or finding their craft sinking.

Castro took advantage of the exodus to clean out the most brutal criminals from his prisons and the most hopeless psychotics from his mental institutions, knowing full well the negative impacts that would weigh on his nemesis, the United States. Sprinkled amid the miscreants and genuine political asylum seekers from Mariel were Cuban spies, the latter dispersing into the fabric of life in Miami.

The games of bolita and street sales of drugs in the 1950s throughout Miami and the Keys exploded as gangs arose and often staged bloody territorial wars. The most organized and violent organizations claimed bigger bites of the pie, and the types of illegal activities widened to include burglaries, prostitution, and extortion. And guess what happened next? From the late 1970s and mushrooming through the 1980s, Miami became the cocaine and ecstasy capital of the world, the major hub of importation from South American cartels either directly or via safe-haven islands in the nearby Bahamas.

Another pal of mine, realtor Jim Catron, who owned a twin-engined plane he kept at a private airport in Fort Lauderdale, made one too many flights between Colombia and Norman Cay in the Bahamas. For reasons still unknown 40 years later, Catron was never heard from again, and no sign of his plane was found. He was sometimes brash and arrogant; I've always thought Catron probably ended up on the wrong side of an AK-47 when contesting payment for a coke flight. Others surmise that his plane simply crashed in the Caribbean and rests in a watery grave.

As explained in chapter 3, my father-in-law at the time, Capt. Grady Patrick, operated a fishing charter business out of Key Largo. He and many other Keys skippers were approached by Cuban American drug dealers offering huge amounts of cash to "cooperate," and some did so. The Marine Patrol, Border Patrol, and Coast Guard vessels off Miami and the Keys were accustomed to the presence of hundreds of charter boats and private boats on the water every day and night. Most of the drugs made it through, and as we know, it didn't help when Coast Guard members based in Islamorada were caught tipping off drug dealers on the whereabouts of law enforcement.

With an influx of almost limitless, mind-blowing volumes of cash—so much so that at times it literally became impossible to count and instead had to be weighed—the corrupting aspect of money influenced the Magic City's political, law enforcement, and judicial systems. Businesses used for laundering money continued to pop up as organized crime leaders came and went.

Aiding and abetting the emergence of Miami's Cuban Mafia was the Tampa Mafia, which took root in the early 1900s and, in the 1930s, was headed first by Santo Trafficante and then starting in the mid-1950s by his son Santo Jr. They expanded its criminal reach with bolita and drug trafficking to the Keys, Miami and Cuba. Representatives of Italian Mafia families throughout the U.S. coexisted and cooperated with other criminal organizations. This became a reality in the casino business especially during the regime of Fulgencio Batista in Cuba in the 1940s and '50s, and with drug lords and cartels in the latter part of the century.

Right in the middle of all this was my company Polytronics International, which as described earned me a good living providing polygraph testing, mystery shopping and eavesdropping services. One of my top employees, John Quarles, left the company at one point due to a cocaine dependency, during which he became heavily involved in the local illicit drug scene. A black man who was not Cuban seldom reached the upper echelons of the Cuban Mafia, but he joined a crew. I reluctantly had to fire him, but when he came out of rehab two years later, I hired him back. He confided to me just how sophisticated the Cuban Mafia operations in Miami were.

"They run things just like a major corporation," said Quarles. "There's the Cuban boss, top-level assistants each overseeing some aspect of the operation, several tough guys with street crews, full-time accountants trying to keep track of the money, front businesses to launder the cash, and an internal security staff. In every sense of the word, it's a Mafia-like criminal organization."

An entity known as The Corporation controlled bolita operations, with offices in Miami and other major cities, run out of New York by former Brigade 2506 member Jose Miguel "El Gordo" Battle Sr., his son Jose Miguel "Migelito" Battle Jr. (released from prison in 2017) and various other members of the Battle family. La Compania, meaning "The Company," is often confused as being synonymous with The Corporation, but it was actually a group that came into being in the late 1990s *competing* with The Corporation; La Compania was headed by Manny Alvarez Sr. and his son Manny Alvarez Jr.

Much of the cash generated by The Corporation flowed to Miami for the purpose of being washed through various front businesses. Confusing law enforcement even more was that many intelligence operatives also referred to the CIA in Miami as La Compania. As noted earlier, after Castro came into power, the CIA occupied a secret field office near downtown Coral Gables—the only domestic office in the U.S. outside Langley, Virginia, its purpose being to train and supply the anti-Castro exile groups, plot assassination attempts on Castro, and monitor Cuban communications in partnership with U.S. Naval Intelligence.

I also employed on a per-job basis a very unusual but interesting fellow who called himself Bill Berry (real name Emil Ernst Behre). Berry did freelance surveillance work, and I got to know him well while hiring him for a few jobs. His background story involved being a former Naval Intelligence officer and hit man, who on an assignment in Central America somehow got bashed in the head, tossed off a dock into the water, and left for dead.

Berry received $400,000 in compensation from the government, he claimed, and in fact he didn't work full-time and owned a nice condo in South Miami as well as a boat and sports car. Though 51 when I knew him, he was a tough Cajun guy and certainly fit the image of a knee buster. Berry also said he'd whacked a few people for the Cuban Mafia and showed me his .22 magnum revolver and hollow point bullets ("I don't like automatics [clip-type handguns] because they tend to jam," he once stated).

After he had regaled me with details about his hits without disclosing any names, I asked Berry why the Cuban Mafia didn't utilize their own crews to kill people.

"They do," he replied, "but they give me some jobs because they think my past government work makes it less likely they'll get pinched by the feds. That's not true, but I'm not going to tell them otherwise—the money is too good."

I quit hiring Berry, a dangerous individual to be around if even half of what he said was true.

Far more credible were my chats with former county managers Ray Goode and the man who succeeded him, Merrett Stierheim. They shared a mutual friendship with Darwin Fuchs, who for decades served as the director of the Miami-Dade County Fair & Exposition. Fuchs, now deceased, loved to fish, and so did Goode and Stierheim, but the two men didn't like each other.

Invited on fishing trips with Fuchs aboard his large catamaran, on some occasions I'd find Goode aboard and at other times Stierheim was there. Both knew of my security background, and in Goode's case he once asked how I reconciled locating clandestine bugs for drug lords. My stock answer was that I'm state licensed and perform a 100 percent legal service, and if I'm certain a client is involved in illegal activities, I'll refuse the job. I did admit that differentiating the good guys from the bad guys isn't as simple as one might think.

Turning the tables, I was just as curious as to how Goode handled the Mafia and organized crime in South Florida as a former county manager and community influencer.

Goode put it quite succinctly: "I dealt with them just as they were rising in power during my tenure [1970 to 1976 as county manager]. At first, I tried to run the county without regard to them, but when people I'd dealt with for years suddenly began stymying anything that might affect the growing drug trafficking that was occurring—even pressuring me to invite some of them to my skybox at the Orange Bowl—I perceived that Miami was headed for some rough times."

Goode was president of the Orange Bowl Committee and a trustee of the University of Miami, which played its football games at the Orange Bowl Stadium, and in its early years so did the Miami Dolphins. During Goode's stint as county manager, the annual Orange Bowl game represented one of the four major NCAA football events and included the Orange Bowl parade, a Miss Orange Bowl contest, and many other county-wide festivities. Goode, therefore, was one of the top movers and shakers in South Florida and somehow kept the Cuban Mafia at arm's length.

Stierheim led the county as manager from 1976 to 1986. Normally far more gregarious than Goode, he didn't speak about the Cuban Mafia or anything resembling civic issues. He came on the outings with Fuchs to fish and relax, and I respected that. However, research reveals that he led the county during ethnic squabbles between whites, blacks, and Cubans. Long after his leaving the manager post, he remained involved in community goings-on, particularly in public relations.

Stierheim did growl that TV shows like *Miami Vice* didn't help the city's image and neither did the "Cocaine Cowboys" label so many referenced as being shoot-'em-up drug lords, especially following the brazen 1979 murders at Dadeland Mall in South Miami. Stierheim's mission became one of reviving the allure that Miami had achieved in prior years as a glittering vacation mecca. His efforts undoubtedly contributed to a tourism revival in the mid- to late 1990s that continues to this day, despite the Covid pandemic. Even so, the Cuban Mafia and drug kingpins continue to be responsible for frequent news articles about gangland murders and busts of traffickers.

Darwin Fuchs put it this way: "People who say the Cuban Mafia here is composed of a bunch of right wingers don't know what they're talking about. Its roots over 50 years ago were based in anti-Castro exiles and trained in the 1960s by the CIA, but most Cubans emigrating here or born here and involved in Mafia activities don't give a rat's ass about political philosophy—it's everything to do with trafficking drugs."

I concur. Any notion that the Miami mob cares if one is a Democrat, Republican, conservative, or liberal is the lot of armchair writers with an agenda. If you've got money or connections, and especially if you have both, the Cuban Mafia will do business with you. The evolution of the Cuban Mafia in Miami is control and taking over other aspects of organized crime like bolita, loan sharking, extortion and prostitution keeps smaller gangs from getting bigger.

Extremists of all stripes exist in Miami, as elsewhere, but to conclude that the Cuban Mafia consists of right wingers is as nonsensical as saying the same of the Italian or Irish Mafia. The rules of every Mafia have nothing to do with who voted for whom in the last election and everything to do with what people bring to the table in terms of earning power or muscle.

Something comical but illustrative of the common knowledge of the presence and prevalence of the Cuban Mafia in Miami slipped from the loose lips of former Miami Police Chief Art Acevedo. Acevedo, hired away from his role as chief in Houston, became Miami's chief of police on April 5, 2021. A little over six months later he was fired. While it's admirable that he wanted to reform the department, stating publicly that the city was controlled by the Cuban Mafia insulted practically everyone, even if they knew it to be true. Acevedo's blunder aside, his remarks confirmed the obvious but ran counter to the bawdy public image the city is forever trying to avoid, even if it's impossible to shed.

For those who'd like to delve into the intricacies of the Cuban Mafia, a must-read is the detailed book by T. J. English titled *The Corporation: An Epic Story of the Cuban American Underworld*. It's nearly 600 pages of fascinating portrayals of myriad organized crime characters, who include many Miamians. Another great read is Avi Bash's *Organized Crime in Miami.*

We can get a glimpse of what's still going on with an incident that occurred prior this writing. In December 2021 a recreational boater in the Keys came across a floating bale containing bricks of cocaine with a street value of over $1 million. Months earlier, the tide washed in another bale containing 25 coke bricks. They obviously became detached from a larger cache awaiting pickup in the Gulf Stream. Had those bales not been accidentally discovered, they would all have ended up in Miami and undoubtedly under the auspices of the Cuban Mafia. One can only imagine how many bales don't get lost.

13

OPERATION EVERGLADES

In 1908 Bert Pacetti of Ponce Inlet, a coastal town just south of Daytona Beach, became a federal bird inspector and game warden. Enormous populations of wading birds such as great white and snowy egrets, flamingos, and roseate spoonbills were being killed each year throughout subtropical Florida to ornament the plumed hats of well-to-do women. President Theodore Roosevelt, his successor President Taft, and the National Audubon Society set out to do something about it, such as naming certain areas federal bird refuges.

Pacetti's family owned a popular hotel in the area bearing their name. He deputized Jesse Linzy, a handyman and fishing guide employed at the hotel, to help ensure that newly established bird reservations weren't still being poached. Topping his list: the Everglades, with swampy interior and shallow coastal estuaries favored by myriad bird species.

Pacetti knew he'd be encountering hardy, resilient people tough enough to survive living among alligators, rattlesnakes, cottonmouths and mosquitos. He definitely didn't anticipate any welcoming committees, and that was why having Linzy by his side would be an intimidating factor.

Linzy, an African American known by his peers as the "Giant of Ponce Park," reportedly stood six feet, eight inches tall with enormous strength— he could easily hoist 100-pound bags of cement mix one-handed without breaking a sweat. But muscle is no match for bullets. Pacetti and Linzy most certainly knew about the 1905 Everglades murder of former bird warden Guy Bradley by a poacher named Walter Smith. It occurred in the appropriately named outpost of Flamingo at the southern tip of Florida's mainland. Nearby Bradley Key is named in his honor.

Through the late nineteenth century until Roosevelt's election, it was legal to hunt and kill plumed birds, resulting in entire rookeries being wiped out. It became a windfall for poor inhabitants of the Everglades who fished, hunted and farmed. An ounce of large plumes earned $20, and that windfall ultimately signed a death warrant for millions of birds annually.

The point of this introduction is that Pacetti, Linzy, and most others intent on putting an end to the poaching came up with little to show for their good intentions. Game management in those days was nearly non-existent and enforcement officers were few and far between. News of the rare forays by lawmen who did venture into the swamp spread quickly, allowing poachers to lie low. Leads sought by interviewing inhabitants of Flamingo and other small coastal towns led nowhere.

Miccosukee and Seminole Indians also felt no interest in helping outsiders. Besides, everyone knew the fate of Guy Bradley and how easily anyone could disappear in the Everglades and never be heard from again. It's a fair bet that a good many murders were blamed on alligators.

The bird onslaught finally ran its course in 1913 when Congress passed the Migratory Bird Act that shut down the New York and London millineries producing the plumed hats.

The next financial windfall for Everglades dwellers didn't take long. Prohibition in the United States kicked in beginning in 1920, and remote coastal settlements like Everglades City on the Barron River—founded in 1923 at the western terminus of the Everglades and located 82 miles west of Miami and about 62 miles south of Fort Myers—became perfect locations to offload booze into the U.S. for truck transport north to Tampa or east to Miami via the nearby Tamiami Trail.

It wasn't until 1929 that the short extension of State Road 29 from the Tamiami Trail to Everglades City was built, making it much faster and more convenient to meet up with the truckers. Collier County in Southwest Florida represented the ideal place to fly under the radar, the most remote portion being the 35,000 acres known as the Ten Thousand Islands.

Dirt-poor residents still existing off fish, game and farming got rich conspiring with bootleggers. Ted Smallwood's trading post in Chokoloskee, a stone's throw to the south of Everglades City, kept locals and visitors—both legit and the criminal-minded—well supplied. Bootleggers rendezvoused with fishing boats just offshore, and the boxes of liquor were hidden in creeks and bays up the nearby East River, Turner River, Lopez River and other coastal tributaries that only locals could navigate without getting lost. To store the booty, covered platforms were erected amid mangrove prop roots that hung out of the water even at high tide.

That generation of inhabitants involved in bootlegging would be mirrored by the same modus operandi decades later when the object of affection became drug trafficking. The quaint placenames of Everglades City and to a lesser extent Chokoloskee and nearby Copeland would no longer

The remote tranquility in and around Everglades City kept it below the radar until law enforcement got wise and raids such as this put an end to it. (floridamemory.com)

be unknown to the world. "Operation Everglades," which kicked off on July 7, 1983, would change everything, creating a local stigma that exists to this day.

"Operation Everglades" isn't exactly original as the name of a federal investigation, but it succinctly describes a drug bust that resonated around the world. For years prior to that day, most of the commercial fishermen in the area who had previously earned subsistence wages selling fish, shrimp, and stone crabs to wholesalers became curiously wealthy.

Things would likely have continued that way were it not for the old Florida Crackers suddenly replacing ramshackle trailers with modern dwellings and swimming pools. Instead of rickety old cars, driveways sported new Cadillacs. Old beat-up boats gave way to sleek vessels that residents couldn't previously have come close to affording. Some started buying parcels of real estate as investments. Investments? That was a word never spoken before Everglades City became a drug port.

At some point in the late 1970s, rumors of this sudden splurge of wealth gradually leaked out until word reached the ears of law enforcement in Naples and Fort Myers. That led to a confluence of local, state and federal efforts to get the skinny on just exactly what was going on. Lawmen knew how clannish the 500 or so residents in that area were, and the planning and execution of the investigations involved years of careful surveillance by air and boat.

In time it all gradually produced a clear picture of just how pervasive and widespread the drug trafficking had become in Everglades City—and the realization that it had been going on unnoticed by law enforcement for nearly five years proved somewhat embarrassing. Besides fishermen, entire families were pitching in to load, unload, and hide the marijuana bales. After the government gathered enough firsthand observations and overheard enough bar talk to identify the co-conspirators, the ax fell.

The evidence showed that just like during the bootlegging years, illegal drugs—in this case seemingly unending bales of marijuana imported directly from Colombia—were being offloaded in Everglades City with a system of handovers. First, freighters from South America would arrive about 50 miles off Everglades City in the Gulf of Mexico. There they would meet large commercial fishing boats in the 60- to 80-foot range and pass bales of pot to the fishing boats. These in turn would rendezvous near shore with a fleet of smaller boats owned by locals.

With all this often taking place under cover of darkness, the skippers stacked and stuffed as many bundles and bales as possible into their boats and turned back to shore. One such boater later said he removed the seats in his boat to make room for more bales, even sitting on a bale to steer. They hid the booty as bootleggers did on platforms they'd built in the shallow upriver mangrove mazes. The odds were almost nil that a casual boater could accidentally traverse the precise river channels and creeks to discover the camouflaged caches. An estimated 300 tons of ganja were being shuttled monthly—*monthly*—from Colombia to Everglades City.

Crabbers, netters, and family fishermen could earn $10,000 per night merely serving as lookouts watching for patrol boats and planes. Vessels offloading bales from freighters might reap hundreds of thousands of dollars, and the layers of runners back to shore upward of $40,000. A system of "it's your turn" allowed the cash to flow to many hands to spread the risk of being caught, and the collusion also compelled co-conspirators to keep their mouths shut.

The federal investigation spanned three years, and a review of the suspects' IRS tax returns didn't come close to matching the extravagant new lifestyles of formerly impecunious fishermen. And so, before the first glimmers of sunlight rose above the swamp on that fateful morning 72 hours after Independence Day in 1983, hordes of federal agents and Collier County deputies raided the towns, immediately arrested 28 locals, and seized half the boats in the region. The Tamiami Trail was blockaded, and same went for the waters surrounding Everglades City, Chokoloskee and nearby Copeland—there was no escape unless one fled on foot into the swamp.

As federal prosecutors are wont to do, they offered plea deals for those willing to talk. At first few did, but once they faced up to 40 years in prison or served time in the slammer, neighbors turned on neighbors, friends turned on friends, relatives turned on relatives. Indictments continued for years, and soon the number of arrests swelled to over 300, meaning that most of the area's population was involved in one way or another in the drug smuggling. As if delivering a final slap in the face, in 1985 the government banned commercial fishing in Everglades National Park.

It does raise a philosophical question. Put yourself in the shoes of someone who knows no other way of life except fishing or hunting in a region not conducive to other opportunities for making a living. You barely get by; your family enjoys a simple existence but never has the finer things in life. Suddenly you're offered twice your annual income for just one night of bootlegging or drug running. Multiply that one night many times over, year after year. Do you succumb to the lure of the happiness and comfort that easy money can buy, especially when many of your friends and even family members are doing so? Most of the people in Everglades City prior to July 7, 1983, rationalized matters that way. Who's to say you wouldn't as well if placed in the same circumstances?

One of the more prominent local characters caught in the bust, Loren Gerome Brown—known by his nickname Totch—was among the few who served time rather than drop the dime on friends and relatives. But that was because he only copped to income tax evasion and received immunity for using his 72-foot trawler to smuggle untold tons of pot. It seems Totch forgot to include on his recent returns over a half million dollars in weed income (at least, that was what he confessed to). He reimbursed Uncle Sam over $1 million and also relinquished about $2 million in niceties to which he'd become accustomed, including a luxury car, a new house, a new shrimp boat, a condo and other expensive chattels.

After serving 20 months of a three-year sentence, Totch returned to Everglades City. Ten years after Operation Everglades, the University Press of Florida published his memoir: *Totch: A Life in the Everglades*. I recall seeing a copy on the desk of the late Biff Lampton in early 1994. Lampton was editor of *Florida Sportsman* magazine at the time, and I the managing editor; we sat across the hall from each other in the publication's South Miami offices. I asked him about the book.

"You've got to read it," said Lampton, who explained that he got to know Totch while serving on Florida's Game & Fish Commission (now the Florida Fish & Wildlife Conservation Commission).

"We knew he and others hidden away at the western edge of the Glades were poaching gators," Lampton disclosed. "I and a fellow officer went to

Chokoloskee to interview him, and he was so delightful that we became friends.

"Totch once told me that he knew I was coming his way before we ever arrived," Lampton laughed. "When asked about poaching gators, a huge grin broke out and he'd say, 'Me? Heaven forbid!' We had no evidence of the poaching, only rumors, and everyone over there we talked to played dumb. We knew the real score, but never could pin anything on Totch. He was a true Everglades personality and I suppose getting caught up in the pot raid probably made him even more of a local legend."

I never met Totch, although we shared the same birthday (March 12). Lampton was killed in a car accident in 1995, and Totch left the world a year later at age 76. But my familiarity with Everglades City and Chokoloskee was just beginning. I served as the tournament director for about 15 years for the Grady Patrick Invitational—Patrick, my then father-in-law, was considered a fishing legend in the Keys. Based at the historic Rod & Gun Club in Everglades City, the event finally disintegrated due to local cheaters entering big fish they'd caught prior to the tournament and walking away with the prize money. We finally wised up and moved the event to Flamingo.

That is of course not to say that everyone is crooked in Everglades City or Chokoloskee—far from it. Present-day folks are quite friendly and accommodating. The Rod & Gun Club still hosts anglers from all over the world, and its past guests include Ernest Hemingway, Thomas Edison, Jimmy Stewart, and John Wayne as well as four presidents: Theodore Roosevelt, Harry Truman, Dwight Eisenhower and Richard Nixon.

Everglades City proclaims itself the "Last Frontier" and the "Stone Crab Capital of the World." It's a cool place to visit, along with Ted Smallwood's store in Chokoloskee, established in 1906 and on the U.S. National Register of Historic Places. I dedicated a chapter to Smallwood in *Florida's Fishing Legends and Pioneers* (University Press of Florida, 2011) and have penned articles in *Florida Sportsman* and other publications about the Ten Thousand Islands and their fabulous light-tackle fishing and excellent seafood eateries.

Even so, Everglades City cannot quite escape a nefarious past involving poaching, bootlegging and drugs. If you do visit, you'll feel more welcomed if you avoid conversations about Operation Everglades.

14

BREACHES IN THE PALM BEACHES

South of the Palm Beaches and north of Fort Lauderdale on the coast is the city of Deerfield. You may recall from an earlier chapter that during Prohibition, Scarface—who'd become a part-time resident of Miami's Palm Island—also opened a commercial fishing business in Deerfield. That made it convenient to bootleg booze from Grand Bahama Island to Deerfield and truck it to Miami and points north as well as to stock his speakeasies and gambling establishments.

Capone's boats were rigged for fishing, to be sure, but each contained a false bottom between the deck and hull to stash boxes of liquor. A hell of a lot more cash was generated by bourbon than by bonito. Just as Capone started the Mafia affectation for South Florida, his Deerfield ventures would precede most other organized crime figures settling from north of Fort Lauderdale to Boca Raton and North Palm Beach. Some of them are portrayed in this chapter, but preceding even Capone by three decades in Palm Beach was a fellow steeped in the casino business, beginning in 1898 and only ending upon his death in 1946.

Edward Riley "Colonel" Bradley grew up during the glory years of the Old West as a cowboy, scout, gold miner and supposedly a pal of Wyatt Earp. He eventually became a successful businessman as a speculator, gambler and racehorse breeder—he owned the Idle Hour Farm in Lexington, Kentucky, where he would ultimately be buried at age 86. His horses won the Kentucky Derby four times and the Belmont Stakes twice. He became involved in bookmaking with several racetracks and owned a hotel in Chicago. Among Bradley's investments: Hialeah Park Racetrack in Miami.

In 1891 Bradley became a realtor in St. Augustine, and seven years later he settled in Palm Beach each winter. He opened the Beach Club on Lake Worth Lagoon, initially with his brother Jack, whom he later bought out. The white wooden edifice housing the Beach Club didn't appear to be extraordinary, but the opulence awaiting inside most certainly did. White

Edward R. "Colonel" Bradley is a legend in Palm Beach, with an extraordinary background as a gold miner, horse breeder and casino pioneer. (floridamemory.com)

and green dominated the interior, with soft lighting that enhanced a re-laxed ambiance and comforting glow.

The clientele consisted of out-of-state high rollers, with each member required to be well groomed and in formal attire. No one could smoke in the gambling rooms, eliminating the choking atmosphere in most casinos of the day. Drinking only took place in the dining room and even then, not to excess. Women could gamble or watch if accompanied by a male member, and the presence of "lady luck" evidently proved to be popular in more ways than one.

Bradley had accumulated so much wealth with his horses and real es-tate deals that at times he'd even reimburse those who lost too much at the tables. Looking for places to park money, he also opened the Palmetto Club as a gambling establishment in New Orleans.

The dining room at the Beach Club seated 212, the menu could match the most elegant restaurants in the nation's biggest cities, and the high prices never deterred his well-heeled members. The Beach Club was con-sidered even fancier and more elegant than the Monte Carlo by those who'd

Bradley's Beach Club operated from 1898 to 1945 and hosted well-heeled gamblers who had to adhere to strict codes of conduct. (floridamemory.com)

visited both casinos. Only the rich and classy became members and adhered to conservative behavior. And just to ensure tranquility, the Colonel employed a security staff of up to 30, all with sidearms. Although seldom encountered, boisterous or boorish behavior resulted in permanent expulsion.

How did Bradley manage to operate a grandiose gambling establishment quite openly in swanky Palm Beach? The way all savvy operators do: by ensuring a flow of copious amounts of cash to local interests. His longtime secretary, Tom Bohne, claimed that Bradley did not bribe politicians or judges, the latter of course being the routine of corruptors, as it had the effect of persuading cops and prosecutors that law enforcement was futile.

However, conflicting reports exist that the Beach Club got raided now and then; but if they are true, it was likely more as a sham show to satisfy the straight-laced set, as no convictions occurred. Such being the case, that made Bohne's pronouncement of bribery innocence a bit dubious. In any event, Bradley and his wife Agnes supported projects for the needy, such as orphanages and hospitals; he treated his staff with the generosity that earns loyalty; and he received no pushback from the local media—in 1934 Bradley bought all the Palm Beach newspapers.

While the Beach Club era ended with Bradley's passing, its longevity for nearly 50 years is quite a testament to his connections and prominence as a Florida gambling pioneer. Future residents of Palm Beach County engaged in illegal activities a far cry more dangerous than Bradley. South Florida—

Fort Lauderdale to Miami to Key West—continued to host the interests of old-school Mafiosi and their cooperation with bolita kings and Colombian and Cuban drug lords. However, the more subdued Palm Beaches began to represent a quieter environment for many Italian mobsters.

Of course, "quiet" doesn't negate the presence of organized crime. Clear evidence of that occurred in 2009 with the arrest of Thomas Fiore of Boynton Beach. Fiore ultimately admitted to operating a crew of 10, and after being suspected of murder, arson, money laundering, extortion and other racketeering crimes, he received a sentence of 12 years.

It was alleged that Fiore and his henchmen formed a wing of the Bonanno crime family. One must wonder how Fiore received a sentence of only 12 years, when he murdered his business partner and burned down a business he owned—the Round One Fitness Center in Royal Palm Beach—in order to collect insurance money. It just goes to show the value of a top-notch legal team that can adroitly negotiate a plea deal.

On August 4, 2016, a federal indictment in West Palm Beach fell on 46 Mafiosi up and down the East Coast with ties to the Philadelphia and Massachusetts mobs as well as the Bonanno, Gambino, Genovese and Lucchese families in NYC. The investigation took five years and involved undercover FBI agents, confidential informants (CIs) and extensive wiretaps.

According to a press release by the U.S. Attorney's Office for the Southern District of New York, FBI Assistant Director-in-Charge Diego Rodriguez stated: "The indictment reads like an old school Mafia novel, where extortion, illegal gambling, arson and threats to 'whack' someone are carried out along with some modern-day crimes of credit card skimming. But the 40-plus arrests of mob associates, soldiers, capos, and a boss this morning show this isn't fiction. As alleged, Genovese, Gambino, Lucchese, and Bonanno LCN [La Cosa Nostra] crime families are still carrying out their criminal activities from Mulberry Street here in New York City to areas of Springfield, Massachusetts. The FBI, working with our task force partners from the New York Police Department, are just as steadfast investigating and rooting out organized crime as wise guys are to bringing it to our streets. We thank all our partners on this multi-year investigation, including the FBI field offices from New Haven, Newark, Miami and Boston for their assistance with operations."

One of the top targets of the 2016 bust was Joseph "Skinny Joe" Merlino, then 54, allegedly considered the boss of the Philadelphia crime family. The succession of bosses in Philly is etched in gangland blood. The boss in the 1960s and '70s in Philly was Angelo "The Gentle Don" Bruno, who was

A clipping dated June 29, 1999, about Joey Merlino, whose part-time residency in the Palm Beaches drew much attention. (Bash Collection)

assassinated in 1980. Next up: Phil "The Chicken Man" Testa reigned until he got blown to pieces the following year. The infamous killer Nicky "Little Nicky" Scarfo took charge until another power struggle occurred in the mid-1990s between Scarfo and both John Stanfa and Merlino.

Merlino's dad, Salvatore "Chuckie" Merlino, worked for Scarfo, and that evidently worked in Joey's favor as he allegedly won out over Stanfa and became the undisputed boss of the Philadelphia family. Scarfo, as has been stated, got pinched for a life sentence and died in prison in 2017.

Merlino had already served most of a 14-year conviction in 2001 for various crimes and, after being released, moved to Boca Raton with wife

Deborah. Being somewhat of a limelight seeker and a spiffy dresser à la John Gotti, in 2014 he served as maître d' for Merlino's, a restaurant owned by a group of investors due to felony convictions preventing anyone from obtaining a liquor license.

Merlino, charged in 2016 with RICO racketeering for gambling and health care fraud—the latter a conspiracy with unscrupulous doctors to bill insurance companies for inflated and unnecessary treatments and medications—resulted in having to post a $5 million bond. He was able to do so using real estate holdings as security and was released to his home with only a GPS ankle monitor.

The trial based on the 2016 indictments took place in NYC. While the other 45 men agreed to favorable plea bargains, Merlino fought the four charges brought against him, and in 2018 a mistrial was declared. He agreed thereafter to plead guilty to one charge of illegal gambling, with the other three charges dropped, resulting in his conviction and a sentence to two years in prison. However, he obtained an early release in 2019 and completed his sentence in a halfway house. It is notable that despite testimony by fellow inmates against him, apparently in exchange for reduced sentences, Merlino stated that he was no longer involved in any criminal activities.

After all Merlino has been through, and being now in his early 60s, one might expect that he would retire and enjoy life. But he ran afoul of the law again, and began serving a two-year sentence while allegedly running Philly family business through Mike Lancelotti, the acting boss. As of this writing, underboss Steve Mazzone is under indictment for racketeering and drug charges. Trying to keep up as to whether Mafia members are active, whacked or imprisoned is a constant challenge.

I do think a possibly redeeming activity Merlino just started as of this writing is a popular podcast that appears on Youtube called "The Skinny with Joey Merlino." It's convincing hearing in his deep voice how he wants to speak on behalf of "all the good guys in prisons who are innocent, particular people of color." Kudos to Merlino if indeed he intends to use his new platform for a worthy cause. Joey, let's do a book together.

Another character of interest arrested in the bust at his home in West Palm Beach was 67-year-old Pasquale "Patsy" Capolongo (a.k.a. "Pat C.," "Mustache Pat," "Fish"). Those bearing the first name Pasquale are typically referred to as Patsy. Capolongo was accused of placing large bets for professional gamblers to hide their identities as well as placing bets of his own. His rap sheet included convictions for gambling and bookmaking, and the feds listed him as a member of the Lucchese family. In a wiretap conversation, Capolongo suggested to an accomplice in New York that he choked a bookmaker who owed Capolongo money and that he threaten death if the fellow tried to stiff him again.

Capolongo claimed he was broke and living off social security. A subsequent search of his residence and a safe deposit box involved in another investigation turned up $526,000 in cash. I wish I was that broke. His relatives secured a $2 million bond and, like Joey Merlino, Capolongo too received only house arrest with a GPS ankle monitor. It forever amazes me how lifelong criminals are not considered flight risks by judges overseeing their cases. Hmm.

In May 2017 Capolongo pled guilty to his 2016 federal indictment in the hope of getting a lighter sentence. As is typical with aging Mafiosi, he claimed in court in NYC on October 3, 2017, before District Judge Richard Sullivan, to be in ill health and retired. His attorney claimed that Merlino now just spent time taking care of his two grandchildren and no longer worked for his brother's landscaping business. Capolongo also boasted that he served time on only two of his 15 gambling convictions, with the other 13 resulting in concurrent time served or fines paid.

It came up in the same hearing before Judge Sullivan that Capolongo had entered a guilty plea in Broward County Court in 2015 for gambling activities, and sentencing was dependent on Sullivan's sentencing. The Broward Sheriff's Office had coordinated with New York investigators, resulting in Capolongo being charged with racketeering, bookmaking, conspiracy to commit bookmaking with offshore betting websites and individuals, and unlawful use of communication with a two-way device (evidently a walkie-talkie).

Sullivan didn't buy Capolongo's defense, stating that his long experience in court and persistent gambling convictions enabled him to play games with the system regarding time served, and that he was beyond being reformed. Also exposed during this hearing were wiretaps in which Capolongo clashed with Merlino because he declined to help Capolongo collect his gambling debts, with each accusing the other of being a rat.

A review of the transcript of Capolongo's day in court on October 3, 2017, reveals how Sullivan and many other judges apply "points" based on the facts of the case and on reviews of reports and testimony submitted by attorneys for the defense and government. In Capolongo's case his attorney was Martin Raskin, and Amanda Kramer was the assistant U.S. attorney.

Sentencing was delayed until proof of Capolongo's claim that despite his 15 convictions, he had served time only twice.

Finally, on March 1, 2018, Sullivan sentenced Capolongo to 18 months prison and supervised release of three years, while dropping the racketeering charges. Sullivan, also overseeing Merlino's case, sentenced him, as stated earlier, to 24 months in prison and one year of supervised release, dropping all the other charges.

As in all parts of the country, in Palm Beach County other major criminal elements continue to plague citizens, business owners, and law enforcement. In February 2022 Police Chief Frank Adderley publicly stated that 18 bad fellas (including a minor) known as the Fourth Street Gang in West Palm Beach were arrested after an 18-month investigation ironically dubbed Operation Goodfellas. Seized in the raids were guns and illegal drugs. The men were charged with attempted murder, gun violations, and drug dealing, activities covering a crime spree of at least 15 years. Their ages spanned 16 to 58, and as of this writing the cases against the gang members are still pending.

The presence of Mafiosi and street gangs notwithstanding, Palm Beach has not lost its effulgence as an upscale town. Visit the exclusive Breakers Hotel and ogle the oceanfront mansions worth tens of millions off Highway A1A. Dress to the nines, stride down Worth Avenue, and hang out with the rich and famous. Who knows, you might cross paths with Donald and Melania.

15

TRAFFICANTE'S TAMPA

The most intriguing Mafia history in Florida is not the Italian gangsters with original roots in NYC, Chicago, Philly and other northern cities who bought second homes in the Sunshine State. Instead, it's about Tampa becoming the focal point of a true homespun Mafia family—and a powerful one at that.

To clear any confusion, you will sometimes read references in the media to Tampa Bay. The body of water separating Hillsborough County's Tampa and Ybor City and other suburbs from Pinellas County's St. Petersburg, Clearwater and Tarpon Springs is indeed Tampa Bay. However, Tampa Bay can also refer to all of Florida's Midwest Coast, encompassing cities in Hillsborough, Pinellas, Manatee and Pasco counties.

For now, let's focus on Tampa in Hillsborough County because that's where Florida's only homegrown Mafia family began. What was to become one of the state's most populated cities took root as Fort Brooke. Built as an outpost by the U.S. Army in 1824 in what is now downtown Tampa, it was intended for dealing with Seminole tribes and later as a military base for the Second Seminole War.

But things seldom went smoothly. Fort Brooke was plagued with soldiers deserting, getting drunk, and succumbing to the charms of prostitutes living in various camps along the Hillsborough River that flows through Tampa. It seemed that the lawlessness and rowdy heritage of Fort Brooke served as a precursor to Tampa Bay's shady reputation well into the twentieth century. Fort Brooke was eventually decommissioned in 1883 and annexed into the City of Tampa in 1907.

As Fort Brooke faded into obscurity, Ybor (pronounced EE-bore) City was just coming into its own. Named after its founder Vicente Martinez-Ybor, beginning in the late 1800s and early 1900s it became the main destination in Tampa Bay for immigrants from Europe, especially Spain and Italy, and from Cuba. Some of the Italian immigrants arrived in the mid- to late 1800s to New Orleans and eventually moved to Ybor City, undoubtedly with some wise guys among them.

Included in Vicente Ybor's vision was a heritage of rolling and manufacturing cigars in Cuba, a country meriting the reputation of growing the finest tobacco in the world. He bought property east of Tampa, named it after himself and built a huge cigar factory. Many other such factories, small and large, popped up in Ybor (often the "City" is dropped) as word reached Cuban cigar workers that life was brighter on the other side of the Gulf Stream. Some immigrants stopped in Miami; others continued to Ybor.

Soon prominent cigar companies flourished in Ybor, like Have-A-Tampa—a play on "Havana" with a U.S. twist—beginning in 1902 to satisfy a nation with millions of tobacco enthusiasts. As the Roaring 20s arrived, pictures in newspapers and newsreels of famous people like President Franklin Roosevelt, Babe Ruth, and even Al Capone puffing on cigars made it seem like the cool thing to do.

As the railroad connected Tampa and Henry Ford's cars came into vogue, a land boom occurred, and Tampa Bay grew in population. Restaurants, shops and markets sprang up along Seventh Avenue, Ybor's main drag, in addition to multiple cigar factories. Social clubs became popular, forming central meeting places for various ethnic groups. Ybor thrived, its distinctive Latin persona taking on nicknames such as Little Havana and Cigar City.

One unsolved mystery pertains to underground tunnels discovered beneath Ybor City that led to the bay. They were built in the late 1800s, but forgotten as time passed only to be accidentally rediscovered in 2018. Some historians surmise that they served as a hidden means to smuggle illegal immigrants into the city or for movement of bootlegged liquor or illegal drugs. Others think the tunnels allowed gamblers to skedaddle if a casino or speakeasy was raided. However, the prevailing view is that they were constructed simply to flush storm water and sewage out of the city and into the bay. Even if that is true, the tunnels nevertheless could still have served for nefarious purposes.

While small-time hoods were already on the scene in Ybor and Tampa to separate people from their property or cash, the first recognized Mafia kingpin was Ignacio Italiano, who died in 1930. After him, Ignacio Antinori rose to power. Originally from Sicily, Antinori built a narcotics network and held power throughout most of the 1920s and in later years with the disputed title of don of Tampa's organized crime. He clashed with others

A prominent political figure and mobster who was once known as the dean of Tampa's underworld, Charlie Wall became a rival of the Trafficantes. (© *Tampa Bay Times*/ZUMA Press)

pushing to be the area's kingpin, most notably Charlie Wall. Antinori had by then secured under his wing the up-and-coming Santo Trafficante Sr., who would become his successor. The friction with Wall became a blood bath that never quite ended until Antinori got taken out with a shotgun blast to the head in 1940. That was when his protégé Santo Trafficante Sr. became the undisputed don, and the Mafia family took on his surname.

Other prominent figures in the early part of the twentieth century turned mainly to drug trafficking. Joseph "Jo-Jo" or "Joe" Cacciatore and Giuseppe "Whispering Willie" Bizzee based themselves in Ybor while building a narcotics network stretching through the southeastern states. Cacciatore and Bizzee got busted in 1925 along with others in their crew. The same thing happened in 1928 when lawmakers nabbed Cuban emigrant George "Saturday" Zarate, who also owned gambling houses. In later years Zarate relocated to New York City, got arrested again on drug charges, and left some bail bondsman holding the bag by fleeing to Cuba, where he lived the rest of his life.

Charles "Charlie" McKay Wall, one of those also arrested along with Zarate in 1928, takes his place as one of the more interesting crime figures in Tampa Bay's history. First, he did not have a foreign heritage. Wall was born and raised in Tampa to a family of wealth and political clout. He came into this world in 1880, his father a doctor who had previously served as the city's mayor, and his mother from a prominent family. Charlie took a liking to Ybor City and befriended its business owners and workers. He had previously opened the Eagle Saloon gambling house in Fort Brooke, and through family connections Wall knew everybody worth knowing in Tampa Bay.

Why he turned to the dark side instead of becoming a respected member of society may be due to an abusive relationship with his stepmother. Others point to a complex borne from his parents regarding him as an underachiever and the black sheep of the family. Whatever the reason, he became a powerful organized crime figure involving bolita, bootlegging, prostitution, and other types of shady activities. As such, he developed ties to criminals of varying ethnicities, including the growing Italian community and Anglos such as himself.

Wall evidently had a keen sense for PR. In 1910 hundreds of cigar employees in Ybor City went on strike, and Wall opened a soup kitchen to help them out. That further endeared him to the Cuban population as well as providing ongoing recognition of his widespread bolita operation. Wall extended his influence by bribing elected and appointed officials, stuffing ballot boxes, and contributing heavily to the campaigns of candidates who could play ball with him. To sum it all up, Wall's net of influence extended widely in Tampa Bay, and he was without doubt one of those contributing to Tampa's reputation far and wide as one of the most corrupt cities in the nation.

But it was seldom smooth sailing for Wall. Friction inevitably developed between Wall, Antinori, and other Italian mobsters who wanted to emulate the growing success of Mafia families up north and all the bootlegging cash being made. Even before Prohibition began in 1920, Tampa Bay—with its myriad tributaries, creeks and docks, like most of Florida's coastlines—became a prime import location for drop-offs of marijuana, cocaine and heroin from South America and the Caribbean.

Bootlegging remained busy even before and after Prohibition, with deliveries of the ingredients for stills to make rum. Thanks in large part to Wall's corruption of the city's legal and political system, arrests and convictions were not anywhere close to proportional to all the criminal activity taking place.

The emergence of Santo Trafficante Sr. in Tampa would inevitably change the entire power structure and, over the years, diminish the clout wielded by Wall. Some of the names on organizational charts of Tampa criminals besides Trafficante included Antinori, Augustine Lazzara, James Cacciatore, Salvatore Italiano (Trafficante Sr.'s underboss), Ignacio Italiano, Joe Vaglica, Jimmy Velasco, Steven Bruno, Jimmy Valenti, the Diecidue clan and Jimmy Lumia. From 1930 to 1959, 25 gangland murders bloodied the streets of Ybor City and Tampa, to be known by historians later as "The Era of Blood." Three of those notable murders involved prominent Mafiosi Antinori in 1940, Velasco in 1948, and Lumia in 1950.

When Lumia got snuffed in 1950, Santo Trafficante Sr. was well established locally with fellow Italian mobsters, and he'd entrenched himself in various business and social organizations. But he recognized that this alone wouldn't win the day in terms of becoming the boss. So he'd already laid the groundwork by courting Mafia leaders in NYC, such as Luciano, as well as dons in Chicago and New Orleans. The tactic succeeded, and soon Trafficante came to recognized as the go-to guy in Tampa.

Born in Sicily in 1886, Santo Trafficante ultimately landed in Tampa just after the turn of the century. He married and started a family that produced four sons, most notably the one named Santo Jr. As the family grew, Trafficante Sr. immersed himself in the local crime scene, especially as it involved bolita, bootlegging during the Prohibition years, and, beginning in the 1940s, involvement in the lucrative drug trafficking trade.

But Trafficante had a vision wider than just presiding over his Tampa Mafia family. He networked with criminal elements in South Florida and visited Cuba, forming a relationship with then dictator Batista. Although already recognized as such by the five NYC Mafia families, by 1950 Santo Trafficante Sr. became the de facto don of what became known far and wide as the Trafficante family—Florida's very own Mafia organization.

The aging Charlie Wall had long before been pushed into the background, and in fact Trafficante Sr. greased that skid by promising Wall freedom from harm if he peacefully bowed out of the scene so as to negate another gangster war. It was an offer he couldn't refuse.

Santo Trafficante Jr. inherited the mantle as don of Tampa's Mafia family from his father, building it into Florida's most powerful criminal organization. (© *Tampa Bay Times*/ZUMA Press)

One of the ways Trafficante Sr. secured his family's dominance focused on helping his son Luigi Santo Trafficante Jr. learn the ropes from the inside. He'd accompanied his dad on trips to Cuba and they both established a friendship with future dictator Fulgencio Batista. In concert with Meyer Lansky, Santo Jr. became one of the most prominent hotel and casino owners in Havana. The mob long recognized Cuba as being an open country free of the increasing hassles from national and state law enforcement agencies and the U.S. government itself.

Under Santo Jr. the family expanded to the point that Mafiosi visiting Florida or doing business in the state first needed to obtain his approval.

A major event unfolded in 1950 when Tennessee U.S. Senator Estes Kefauver began public hearings in various cities across the nation that exposed the extent of organized crime. One of the hearing sites: Tampa. The Trafficantes avoided testimony by taking up temporary residence in Cuba, but Charlie Wall made the tragic mistake of agreeing to testify. In doing so, Wall put his resentment of the Trafficante family in the center of the bull's-eye, which called into question the tax returns of Santo Sr. and Jr., among others. Evidently believing that Trafficante Sr.'s word of nonviolence a decade earlier was still binding, Wall even took to badmouthing the Trafficantes around town, including racial slurs about Italians.

When Santo Sr. died from cancer in 1954, Santo Jr.—who was not a party to any oath of protection for Wall—likely retaliated as the family's boss. On April 18, 1955, Wall's throat was cut and his head was hammered flat with a blackjack, according to a police file. Sown over his body was bird seed, and with it a copy of Kefauver's book *Crime in America,* which included Wall's testimony. While the identity of Wall's killer remains a mystery, most historians suspect Santo Jr. ordered it.

Although his dad didn't die until 1954, Santo Sr.'s health took a dive years beforehand, and by 1950 Santo Jr. had already taken over most of the family business and was widely regarded as the undisputed don of Tampa's Mafia. While he was considered quiet and polite in dealing with people, few dared to challenge Santo Jr.'s authority, and he was able to bring local bolita dealers under his wing—those who refused mysteriously disappeared.

Even so, most of the 1950s ensued with little gangland warfare and few sanctioned hits. Santo Jr. expanded his interest in bolita and gambling into South Florida and the Keys and owned a home in Miami. He established narcotics trafficking deals in Southeast Asia and with the Colombian cartels. Money flowed heavily from the family's gambling interests in Cuba. In essence, the path his dad had blazed became a full-blown highway under Santo Jr.'s authority. Santo Sr., cut from the cloth of traditional Sicilian Mafiosi, produced a second Trafficante generation more in the mold of a modern don.

When Castro came to power and booted out the Mafia, Santo Jr. did a short stint in prison there—the only time he ever served behind bars de-

spite an entire life of major criminal activity. He did get convicted of bribery in 1954, but the Florida Supreme Court overturned it. He ultimately
beat all other charges or indictments with a wily legal team headed by attorney Frank Ragano. Facing trials at the age of 72 and in ill health, Santo
Jr. died in 1987 during heart surgery. He left behind two daughters and wife
Josephine, who lived until age 95. He also left behind a Mafia family that
had seen better days.

After being released from prison and expelled from Cuba, Santo Jr. resided in Miami with Josephine and the daughters for several years while
still controlling the Tampa family. He cavorted with other South Florida
Mafiosi as well as anti-Cuban militants, and according to declassified documents had once conspired with the CIA to poison Castro.

One of the biggest controversies surrounding Santo Jr. is that he was one
of those behind the assassination of President Kennedy—an accusation he
always denied. The Mafia certainly wanted John Kennedy killed after his
brother Bobby, as U.S. attorney general, harassed the mob, especially Chicago boss Sam Giancana. Giancana felt betrayed after allegedly swinging
the Illinois vote to JFK in the 1960 presidential election.

What role, if any, Santo Jr. and his henchman played in JFK's murder
will likely never be known, especially since conspiracy theories include
blaming Castro (in revenge for all the CIA plots to kill him) and the Soviet
Union (in embarrassment over the Cuban missile crisis in 1962). Angles
adding to the latter theory were that Lee Harvey Oswald formerly lived
in Russia, spoke the language fluently, married a Russian woman and was
rated a rifle marksman in the military.

As history recorded on live television, Jack Ruby, a crime figure in Dal-
las, killed Oswald a couple of days after his arrest, supposedly to hide the
Mafia's involvement in the assassination. The mob theory is enhanced by
reports of a witness that Ruby visited Santo Jr. when the latter was in the
Cuban prison. Others allege that the CIA and Lyndon Johnson were behind it. I personally doubt that Oswald acted alone, given all those possible
scenarios. Considering the abundant connections between the Trafficante
family in Tampa, the Marcello family in New Orleans, and Giancana in
the Chicago Outfit, I'd put my money on the Mafia's involvement in JFK's
assassination—and that some elements in the CIA knew about it.

Recently a letter has appeared in Oswald's handwriting dated two weeks
prior to JFK's assassination and addressed to a "Mr. Hunt." Many believe
him to be E. Howard Hunt, a CIA operative involved in JFK's ill-fated Bay
of Pigs invasion and who was to be a future Watergate burglar.

The letter states, "Dear Mr. Hunt, I would like information concerding my position. I am asking only for information. I am suggesting that we discuss the matter fully before any steps are taken by me or anyone else. Thank you, Lee Harvey Oswald." The misspelling of "concerning" turned up in another letter Oswald wrote, giving credence to the Hunt letter's authenticity.

Another controversy is the claim that Santo Jr. may have been behind the NYC murder in 1957 of Albert "The Executioner" Anastasia in the barber shop of the Park Sheraton Hotel. Santo Jr., visiting NYC at the time, checked out of his hotel just prior to the murder. It was known that bad blood existed between him and Anastasia. Then again, I once left NYC the same day mobster Joe Gallo was murdered, and I obviously had nothing to do with it. The connecting-the-dots game regarding Santo Jr.'s involvement in the death of Anastasia is therefore unconvincing.

Still another alleged dot connection took place when Santo Jr. had dinner with Chicago Mafioso Johnny Roselli. The following day, Roselli didn't make it to a golf outing. It seems that Roselli angered many in the mob by testifying about mob involvement in the Kennedy assassination and conspiracies with the CIA to kill Castro. Roselli's body was ultimately found in a 55-gallon drum in Biscayne Bay, and no one ever got charged for the hit. Perhaps having dinner with Santo Jr. could be hazardous to your health, because the same happened to Miami mobster Lou Coticchia: The day after he dined with Santo Jr., Coticchia disappeared.

After Santo Jr.'s death, the vibrancy of the family indeed dissipated. Among the likely reasons: The state started a legal lottery in 1988 that put a major hole in bolita action; many of the old-time Mafiosi were dead or elderly; snitches began cooperating more than ever with law enforcement agencies and prosecuting attorneys; prison sentences for drug trafficking had increased dramatically; law enforcement agencies quit competing for media glory and started sharing intel; and many offspring of mobsters recognized all those factors and decided to avoid a criminal career. There are still active Mafia families in various cities, but likely far less powerful than in days of old.

Fragments of Mafia presence persisted in Tampa. Frank Diecidue, who had served for many years as Santo Jr.'s underboss, didn't get the nod, and instead Vincent Salvatore LoScalzo allegedly became don and shared power with Frank Albano. Other mobsters of varying prominence active before and after them included Nick and Al Scagglione, Frank Ippolito, John Remmi, Louis Figueredo Sr. and Jr., Jim Donofrio, Angelo Bedamy Sr., and scores of others. The big questions are who's in charge of the Tampa Mafia these days and, if it exists, how prominent is it? Some say it's been absorbed by NYC's Gambino family, and according to Tampa Mafia historian Scott Deitche, there may be a few wise guys operating here and there in Tampa, but not anything close to what prevailed during its prior heyday.

In seeking definitive answers, I made a Freedom of Information Act request to the FBI and the Florida Department of Law Enforcement as to the succession of leadership in the Tampa Mafia since Santo Jr.'s death. The FBI declined to provide anything, claiming that my FOIA request was too broad. However, it seems unlikely the FBI doesn't have any records pertaining to who now runs the Tampa Mafia or if it exists. The FDLE replied but provided nothing definitive.

Ybor City, the birthplace of Tampa Bay's Mafia, floundered in the latter half of the twentieth century as the adverse medical effects of tobacco became known—most notably lung cancer. That put a major dent in the cigar, cigarette, and chewing tobacco industries. Ybor City began to lose its mojo, and its brick buildings and warehouses that once served as vibrant workstations to hundreds of cigar makers sat empty for over two decades. As commerce shrank, so did tourism.

Fortunately for Ybor City, a major revival occurred in the latter half of the century—it's now a National Historic District—and today it offers trendy millennial bars and cool eateries along Seventh Avenue and cross streets. The city's anchor was and still is the famed Columbia Restaurant founded in 1905, which serves as a magnet for locals and tourists enamored with its Latin cuisine and Flamenco shows.

Tampa's bar scene has also been notorious for strip clubs (often calling themselves "gentlemen's clubs") in Ybor City and along a section of Tampa's main drag, Dale Mabry Highway. In the early 1970s I met with an attorney friend named Phil Beck from Lakeland when visiting Tampa for a grand jury hearing about Watergate, in which I was a witness. Neither of us was married at the time.

Beck looked up his old University of Florida pal Gene O'Steen and we met him one night at 2001 Odyssey on Dale Mabry directly across from the infamous Mons Venus strip club. O'Steen showed us his office in the club and we witnessed thousands of coins scattered about and numerous bags and crates of coins. He informed us that his vending machines selling cigarettes and offering arcade games yielded a constant flow of income.

I've seen no evidence directly connecting O'Steen to being a member of organized crime, but a career owning and operating strip clubs in Tampa

James Costa "Jimmy" Longo (*left*) served as Santo Jr.'s bodyguard, driver and hit man and is shown here with attorney Frank Ragano. (© *Tampa Bay Times*/ZUMA Press)

and the fact that for decades the Mafia controlled the vending machine business nationwide certainly suggests some sort of cooperative relationship.

For a time O'Steen partnered with Jose Manuel Garcia and they accumulated a coterie of strip clubs in the 1970s. At one point it's been reported they sold some of them to Caesar Rodriguez with the agreement that O'Steen and Garcia would retain the vending income. That arrangement may have resulted in conflict with hit man Sam Cagnina III and drug trafficker Victor Manuel Acosta. Both Garcia and Rodriguez had their cars blown up, and Cagnina and Acosta are suspected of having had something to do with it. How O'Steen managed to navigate safely amid dealing with dangerous characters like them is a credit to his personality and business acumen.

I got to know O'Steen a bit when he accompanied Beck and me to Panama. A friend of mine named Jim Malone owned shrimp boats, and I thought O'Steen might be interested in owning a percentage of one or more of the shrimp boats. It didn't pan out, but I found O'Steen to be a really cool and likable guy. He passed away in 2022 at the age of 82.

When delving into Tampa's Mafia history, one of the first things I did was to call my cousin Suzanne in Tampa. Suzanne's mother Ruth was one of my dad's sisters. Suzanne married a very cultured, dignified fellow named Vince Longo in 1961, whose uncle was a well-known made man in the Trafficante family: James Costa "Jimmy" Longo. Jimmy served as Santo Jr.'s bodyguard until the 1970s and at times as his driver.

Jimmy was muscular and emitted the essence of a man you didn't want to mess with. He worked off and on at the Columbia Restaurant in Ybor City, a favorite eatery of the Trafficantes and often the scene of shared dinners with visiting Mafiosi. For purposes of washing money and the appearance of being a legit member of society, Jimmy at one time or another owned a bowling alley and a car repair garage. He also served as the Tampa mob's representative with other national Mafia families when it came to coordinating gambling interests.

I called Suzanne about recollections of Jimmy in the hope of gleaning some interesting tidbits about the Trafficante family. Suzanne told me that over the years at Jimmy's invitation she and Vince attended social events thrown by Santo Jr. and other local Mafia members, but no one talked business at those gatherings and nobody asked questions. She added that everyone they met at such occasions was always polite and friendly. So much for getting inside info.

I also reached out to my son-in-law, who does contracting work for Henry Trafficante, but that line of inquiry also hit a brick wall. Trafficante declined an interview, citing a disdain for gratuitous media scrutiny. Can't say I blame him—that's the credo of any wise wise guy.

Regarding LoScalzo allegedly becoming don of the Trafficante family post-Santo Jr. in 1987, it's known that he served as one of the drivers for Santo Jr. Besides numerous ties to fellow Italian mobsters in other states, LoScalzo owned a number of bars and restaurants. His criminal interests were broad, including the fencing of stolen property, hijacking, and drug trafficking.

LoScalzo was arrested for and convicted of various crimes over the years, and a serious dent under his alleged watch involved 18 members of the Trafficante family in Miami getting busted in 2000, including Steven Raffa, the main Trafficante representative in South Florida. More indictments followed in ensuing years, further diminishing not only the Trafficante family but also criminal organizations in other cities.

The Trafficantes certainly left their mark on Tampa Bay's history, a remnant of the more active years of *La Cosa Nostra* nationwide. Scott Deitche's best-selling book *Cigar City Mafia* is highly recommended.

16

CRACKER COWBOYS

I decided when formulating the chapters for *Sunshine State Mafia* that I'd do justice to each area of the state regarding Mafia history. Within the limits of one book, it has proven to be easier said than done. That would mean some chapters would merit modest length while others, like South Florida and Tampa Bay, would occupy more pages. But that's as it should be, as regional competition for being under Mafia control is hardly a noble accomplishment.

Prior to 1971 interior counties surrounding Orlando from Lake Okeechobee to Ocala depended mainly on the commerce of cattle ranches and orange groves. Occasional rustlers, poachers, and burglars caught in the act were generally handled by local sheriffs or just as often by revengeful residents accustomed to treating miscreants as they saw fit.

Taking the law into your own hands sometimes made for the only recourse in that many rural areas possessed little in the way of law enforcement equipped to deal with anything more than speeding tickets, drunks and petty crimes. Forensic science and DNA analysis just weren't around then, and the pay rate for rural cops was a joke. Paying off whoever existed in the way of lawmen or the judiciary was almost as commonplace as getting off the hook just by way of being blood related or former school chums.

Organized crime still reared its ugly head in all portions of the state to varying degrees, including Central Florida. Bootlegging and personal stills kept the booze flowing during Prohibition, and illegal drugs could be obtained from small-time dealers here and there or by visiting a nearby city, but what really became a lucrative vocation for organized crime focused on bolita—the widespread illegal game of chance mentioned in several previous chapters.

Ranch hands, grove pickers, gas station attendants, store clerks and the like showed no inhibitions about trying their luck at a nice payday for relatively small wagers. But add it all up when you have the organization to

Harlan Blackburn (*seated at far left*) started a life of crime as a member of the Dixie Mafia and became Central Florida's most prominent gambling kingpin. (floridamemory.com)

gather thousands of bets each day and the payoffs become extremely lucrative. All that was just the way it was before the state decided to get into the gambling business with the statewide lottery in 1988. Online sports betting would deliver another blow to bolita years later.

But those "legal" games didn't exist in the 1950s, and up until the '70s a loosely coordinated group known as the Dixie Mafia (also called the Southern Mob or Cracker Mob) was based in Biloxi, Mississippi. It controlled racketeering in rural areas of the southeastern United States, including some thinly populated portions of Florida. In most cases they raked in revenue via fenced stolen goods.

The Dixie Mafia consisted of what some would term southern rednecks, who in our state were more politely termed Florida Crackers, although a better description would simply to call them a bunch of tough guys with no strict hierarchy like that of *Cosa Nostra* families. In some areas, however, like Mississippi and Louisiana, the Dixie Mafia did at times operate with efficiency, with illegal activities often carried out by former convicts who possessed considerable criminal experience. Besides stolen goods, the Dixie Mafia dabbled in a wide range of crimes including drug dealing, prostitution, burglary, and selling liquor in many southern counties that stayed dry even after Prohibition. Snitchers got their asses kicked if lucky and got whacked if not.

However, the real cracker kingpin in Florida throughout the 1950s and '60s was Harlan "The Colonel" Blackburn. An Orlando resident, he joined the Dixie Mafia at an early age and proved to be a major earner—the sure pathway toward upward mobility in a criminal organization. Ed Milam, a fellow who'd been running the Central Florida group but who'd fallen under a 10-year probationary period for running bolita in Polk County, found himself on the wrong end of a gun one day in 1953. His body turned up in a ditch south of nearby Kissimmee, although evidence seemed to indicate that Milam was killed elsewhere and his body dumped in the ditch to hide the murder scene.

Blackburn took over, causing many to wonder if he was behind the Milam murder to gain control, but the killer's ID evaded capture. However, it could well have been someone other than Blackburn because Milam had not endeared himself to those already involved in the Central Florida bolita rackets due to his propensity for taking overly generous cuts of the

Bolita balls and tickets. The illegal game proved highly popular in Florida before the lottery came into being, and Blackburn's organization reportedly raked in well over $100,000 per week off thousands of regular bettors. (Tampa Bay History Center)

booty for himself. That rattled colleagues, many of whom had been placed by Milam into top positions in the organization.

Even before all that bedlam with Milam, Blackburn was on thin ice after he and some of his gang members were arrested a number of times in three Central Florida counties, in addition to his gambling rap in nearby Polk County. Dazed by the unwanted heat, Blackburn nonetheless continued to build the bolita business through the rest of the 1950s and 1960s, and his list of regular customers numbered in the thousands. Many bolita gamblers wagering under a buck and even just a few cents would play every day, and yet the weekly take ran between an estimated $100,000 and $200,000.

Do the math and you can visualize just how massive a following Blackburn enjoyed. His group included lieutenants who would visit the numerous locations where the bolita tickets were being sold to collect the bets. They would also pay off winners, and that was when the opportunity arose for a crooked bet collector to pay himself a winning amount even if he hadn't collected a real bet. He'd simply make out a ticket to a co-conspirator or a fictitious name after the bolita number was chosen. It's a gambit that can only be done occasionally so as not to draw suspicion.

The only Dixie Mafia groups outside Florida that dealt with the Italian Mafia were those near Louisiana, due to the influence of the Marcello family in New Orleans. Even then it was on a small scale. Florida was an exception to that, however, because Blackburn realized that no one did business of any magnitude in the Sunshine State without the consent and if desired the participation of the Trafficante family in Tampa. Blackburn formed a partnership with Trafficante soldier Salvatore "Sam" Cacciatore, which gave Blackburn the unmistakable reputation that you'd better not cross him.

Things bumped along quite nicely for years for Blackburn and his crew with the backing of the Trafficantes. The cash poured in nonstop. On occasion Blackburn would get pinched for a gambling charge here and there and receive short stints in the slammer just so that the local gendarmes could pretend they were doing their jobs. In fact, the cops never even put a dent in the weekly take.

Happy times took a major nosedive for Blackburn in 1971. It occurred because of the need to evade wire taps that law enforcement sometimes obtained for phone booths, as they knew that that was how the bad guys often communicated. It was exactly what Blackburn arranged with Clyde Lee, who worked for him. As Lee stood in his phone booth, he sustained four bullet wounds when a car pulled up and someone sprayed him. Minutes later someone pulled up and attempted to do the same to Blackburn at his booth on the other end of Orlando, but supposedly a milk truck got in the way and the gunman sped away without firing a shot.

Sam "The Fat Man" Cagnina, a veteran Trafficante member, somehow got charged for the attempted hit on Lee, who survived and evidently provided testimony too vague to convict Cagnina. The twist was that Cagnina beat the rap but Blackburn didn't, getting convicted for masterminding the assault on Lee.

The likely scenario is that Blackburn suspected Lee of going south with some of the bolita cash and, as an alibi, pretending he had also been assaulted in another booth. The jury certainly didn't buy into the fairy tale of a milk truck fortuitously appearing and thwarting a hit man.

Blackburn received a serious sentence and went to the slammer for a few years before regaining his freedom in the mid-1970s. The Trafficantes most likely took over the reins, but by then they had become more focused on allocating their time to serious drug dealing because that income stream made the bolita dough look like chump change. As mentioned in the last chapter, Santo Trafficante Jr. had set up deals with large cartels in South America and Southeast Asia that could grow thousands of acres of plants, harvest them, and refine the marijuana, cocaine, heroin and other chemical extracts of value in their labs.

The Trafficantes provided transit of the illegal narcotics into the United States and trafficked them to points north. They kept a semblance of the bolita action coming in so as to thwart competition, but the profits being made by distributing the cartel drugs were so enormous that even washing it became a gargantuan challenge.

Many gangsters, when they sniff clean air for the first time after being let out of prison, pledge to go straight. Blackburn was no exception and said so publicly in 1992, but as with so many others singing that tune, the lure of easy money soon recaptured his attention. The Florida lottery had already cranked up and was taking a bite out of bolita proceeds. Disney World had turned the former cow town of Orlando into a bustling city with a huge tourism trade. As a city's population grows, so does the budget for larger police departments to handle higher rates of crime.

Blackburn evidently read those tea leaves but, forgetting his pledge to become a do-gooder, listened instead a bit too much to someone like Cacciatore extolling the benefits of getting a piece of the illegal drug money gravy train. Blackburn went about setting up a drug organization in Central Florida, and his naïveté resulted in carelessly bringing into the fold a government confidential informant. However it went down, Blackburn got smacked by the IRS when he couldn't account for all the cash he'd been hauling in, and as the government was wont to do in order to discourage other would-be drug lords, law enforcement slapped Blackburn with a hefty 20-year sentence.

Already 73, Blackburn died in prison in 1998, a sick man who likely kicked himself every day for not comfortably retiring and instead chasing the cocaine lure of beaucoup Ben Franklins.

17

PROBLEMATIC PANHANDLERS

On occasion my South-Florida-based security consulting company would line up enough clients in other regions for us to put together a statewide route. During one such trip that found me in Daytona Beach at a huge tiki bar on its famous beach in the late 1980s or early '90s, I sat at the counter in view of one of the cash registers. As I sipped a Capt. Morgan and cola, an angry barrage shot from the mouth of one of two men seated near me.

The talker's accent gave away a heritage from New York or Jersey, and I focused my ears on him amid the soothing sound of breaking surf and a fellow doing an off-tune version of "A Pirate Looks at Forty" at the band-stand.

The loud man at the bar counter had a swarthy complexion, glasses and dark hair. Events not to his liking were taking place, specifically something about "rats shooting their mouths off" and making life miserable for him and his family. While short in stature and hunched over on his stool, the guy nonetheless emitted an intimidating persona, even though at the time I didn't view him as being violent or inebriated. The man sitting next to him scurried away, leaving a seat open between me and the boisterous fellow.

He noticed me looking at him and, with both hands open and palms pointed upward, asked, "Am I being too loud?"

I smiled. "No, I'm intrigued though. What's on your mind?"

He stared at me a moment, smiled, then moved next to me. "I am pissed about a lot of things," he continued, "but I know a stranger's problems are boring to most people."

"Well, I'm a lot more bored just sitting here by myself, so I'd be up for some interesting chat."

My interest had less to do with what he said than with using him as a cover. When doing a mystery shopping, the best way to seem inconspicuous to sharp-eyed bartenders is to appear uninterested in the goings-on behind the counter. That worked out nicely if seated in a position to talk to someone while also glancing over the person's shoulder to keep track of how drinks were poured and checks rung, and if any cash payments ended up anywhere except the register drawer.

My new bar buddy didn't introduce himself. Instead, he launched into a rambling dissertation about loyalty and how some people make pledges of discretion and then break them. Though intense, as I described, he wasn't threatening. But the main objects of his ire for the next five minutes or so centered on John Gotti and several others with Italian names I don't recall. Even I knew that Gotti was the famed Teflon Don of the Gambino family. This guy sure seemed to be quite familiar with *La Cosa Nostra.*

At that point I couldn't help myself. "Who are you?" He flicked a brief smile and looked me dead in the eyes.

"Believe me, you're better off not knowing." With that he paid his tab and left without even shaking hands. Evidently my asking even one question ended the one-way conversation.

I forgot about that incident until many years later, when I read an old article about Paul Castellano being murdered outside Sparks restaurant in NYC in 1985, and how that hit hadn't been previously cleared with the permission of the other family bosses. With Castellano out of the way, John Gotti took over as boss of the Gambino family. Several other gangsters were pictured in that story, including Anthony "Gaspipe" Casso.

I swear to this day it was Casso himself, the same guy with the glasses, acne, and dark hair, letting off steam at a Daytona Beach bar counter. The only difference was that his picture showed him with a mustache. Reading that story, I found out that Casso rose to be boss of the Lucchese family, possessed a rep as a psychotic killer, and would eventually receive a life sentence of 455 years for multiple murders. He died in prison in 2020.

Good Lord, I may have been seated next to a mobster feared even by other mobsters. It also jogged my memory of seeing the frightful Aniello Dellacroce at Mutiny Bay during a mystery shopping.

Admittedly a college degree in psychology doesn't qualify me for accurate analyses—particularly from brief encounters—but if indeed that was Casso, he seemed quite sane to me. Then again, I wouldn't want to meet him if I'd crossed an *omerta* loyalty oath and was talking to the feds. While organized crime in North Florida as well as in the northwest part of the state—in the Panhandle from Tallahassee to Pensacola—hasn't been nearly as prominent as in South Florida and Tampa, it's certainly deserving of a chapter of its own.

In March 2021 the Jacksonville Sheriff's Office arrested Hakeem Robinson for a 2019 murder, and the detectives likely believe he was responsible for others. He was already in prison along with his dad, Abdul Robinson, when both were arrested in 2020. According to the Jacksonville Sheriff's Office (JSO), Abdul ran a drug ring for decades known as ATK, which some believed stood for "Ace's Top Killers."

Gangs have become prominent in northeastern Florida, particularly Jacksonville and Daytona Beach. According to a report by the JSO, at least 30 gangs have been active in the city, with gang territorial disputes and related violence becoming more prevalent. Gangs certainly qualify as organized crime, and some are very well organized. Besides dominating street crimes, the main gang focus and income stream involves narcotics trafficking—what else is new.

In 2011 the U.S. attorney's office in Jacksonville indicted members of the Guardians gang. The charges included bank and home robberies, extortion, and distribution of oxycodone, steroids and cocaine. In 2015 a JSO officer was among 13 arrested in Operation Thunderstruck, conducted by the Organized Crime Drug Enforcement Task Force with agencies such as the IRS, ATF, Secret Service and others. So many acronyms, so little time. The gang conspired in activities like drug trafficking and money laundering that involved hiding proceeds from questionable car purchases and depositing less than $10,000 at a time into various banks to avoid IRS scrutiny.

In 2018 members of the Rolling 20s gang were indicted by the U.S. attorney's office in Jacksonville on gun charges and drug trafficking. This investigation brought together the ATF and the JSO.

In July 2022 deputies arrested former state correctional officer Christina Guest and others in a drug trafficking ring after an investigation by the FBI and the Volusia Bureau of Investigation. Methamphetamines were being distributed and sold in Volusia County, which includes Daytona Beach, as well as in nearby Lake County north of Orlando.

And so it goes. While Mafia influence has sunk, as is seemingly the case throughout most of the U.S., organized crime in all its ugly forms never seems to be totally stoppable.

From Tallahassee to Pensacola, its crime history consists of rural racketeering carried out by members of the Dixie Mafia in the 1950s and '60s. A more consistent nuisance involves gangs of teenagers who carry out crimes such as auto burglaries—good lord, lock your car doors, people—shoplifting, and drug possession.

According to the sheriff's department in Okaloosa County, in the cities of Destin and Fort Walton Beach four gangs operated composed mainly of teens. In one case a turf war between two gangs brought about a shooting.

Busts such as this that occurred years ago in Tallahassee are becoming more prevalent due to the rise of violent drug gangs in North Florida and the Panhandle. (floridamemory.com)

Retail theft rings became prevalent, typically consisting of two or more thieves entering selected retail outlets and stealing targeted items that are easy to sell online. One small local retailer alone estimated recent shoplifting losses amounting to $20,000.

The DEA reports that a far more threatening specter is the expansion of Mexican drug cartels in the U.S., known specifically as Mexican Transnational Criminal Organizations (TCOs). They tend to push out other drug traffickers and criminals by initially offering to become involved with their operation, which results eventually in taking over—a refusal to cooperate invites a long walk off a short pier.

A remarkable execution-style double murder occurred in the Panhandle in 2009. Byrd "Bud" Billings, 66, and his wife Melanie Billings, 43, were in their rural home with nine of their 16 children present. Each parent operated a used car lot. Bud also owned a financial services company and previously a strip club.

It was reported that those arrested in the murders mentioned a connection to the Mexican Mafia but didn't want to testify for fear of being killed. I didn't see that in the court records, but it did appear in some media outlets. The part possibly involving the Mexican Mafia was that scams were taking place in the Panhandle that involved theft from used car lots and those cars being sent to Mexico. It appeared that the Mexican Mafia somehow got screwed out of a large sum of money and therefore had a motive to commit the Billings murders. That was not how things panned out, however.

Byrd and Melanie Billings had two children from previous marriages and adopted 12 children, with most being special needs kids. They had a large home in the suburbs west of Pensacola that housed their large family. Byrd Billings provided loans and did so for local resident Leonard Patrick

Leonard Patrick Gonzalez Jr. is serving time for masterminding a murder-robbery in 2009 that shocked everyone in Pensacola. (Florida Department of Corrections)

Gonzalez Jr. The latter started a karate dojo (martial arts training center) with the loan. His relationship with the Billingses somehow soured, and Gonzalez—with a previous rap sheet for burglary—believed a safe in the Billings home contained millions of dollars in cash.

Gonzalez, 35, hatched a detailed plan to break into the Billings's residence and rob the safe with the help of eight others, including his father who drove one of the two getaway cars. On the evening of July 9, 2009, Gonzalez Jr. and accomplices dressed in black ninja outfits stormed the Billings's house while nine of their children were present.

Gonzalez demanded that Byrd open the safe, and when he refused, Gonzalez shot him in one leg, then the other, and finally executed him when the denials continued. Gonzalez next shot and killed Melanie. None of the children was harmed. Shell casings were found at the scene, and the accompanying handgun was later traced to one of the gang members.

Unfortunately for the conspirators, the Billingses had 16 security cameras all around the home, which captured the entire assault and the murders. The gang removed the safe and later opened it remotely, only to discover it contained but a few pieces of jewelry, medications and personal documents. Another safe in the home did contain a large amount of cash, but the perpetrators didn't find it. Subsequent attempts by Gonzalez and the others to cover up their involvement failed, and prosecutors armed with the security camera evidence used it to flip some of the co-conspirators to testify against Gonzalez.

In the ensuing trial in October 2010 eight people were convicted for the planning of and participation in the crime. Sentencing in February 2011 came down with Gonzalez Jr. now serving two death penalty sentences for the first-degree murders and a life sentence for home invasion with a firearm, which was reconfirmed in 2014 by the Florida Supreme Court. Two others received life sentences, and the rest got long stretches in prison. Two of the conspirators died in prison in 2015, including Gonzalez Sr.

That event represented one of the most heinous crimes in the Panhandle's history. It was a foreshadowing of things to come in terms of the Mexican Mafia and cartels becoming active in Florida, even in rural areas. For example, in 2021 a block of synthetic opioid was found in Marion County that brazenly contained a stamp on it of a sombrero and the word "Mexico." In Flagler County a kilo of fentanyl turned up in a private home during a drug raid with a potency capable of killing 500,000 people. Usually, fentanyl is in a powder form, but it can also be adulterated in over-the-counter pills to hide its true nature.

The DEA reports that the discovery of such counterfeit pills has risen 430 percent and that U.S. Customs and Border Protection stats reveal that seizures of fentanyl at the Mexican border more than doubled, rising from 4,791 pounds in 2020 to 10,469 in 2021. The Miami DEA stated that fentanyl is being smuggled into Miami and other cities by sea, by air, and even in the mail from Mexico. The openness of the Mexican border in recent years is also considered a contributing factor for the explosion of fentanyl with the Mexican Mafia and cartels behind it. Fentanyl is relatively inexpensive, it's far more powerful than other opioids, and it's in high demand.

The Mexican Mafia is suspected of operating in Florida urban areas as well. It seems that as the American version of *La Cosa Nostra* is shrinking, the void is being filled by organized criminals of other origins, such as Cuban, Mexican, Russian, and even Chinese. Our law enforcement agencies—already overwhelmed—will have to adjust accordingly to the rise of the Mexican Mafia, and prosecutors must likewise become more aggressive.

18

THE GOOD GUYS

Okay, it's a given that *La Cosa Nostra* is not the same as in the days of Luciano, Costello, Genovese, Lansky, Gambino or even Gotti. The old guard embraced the essence of *omerta,* but that was when they could operate much more clandestinely. In its heyday the Mafia may well have been "bigger than U.S. Steel," as Meyer Lansky once bragged, but it's not so any longer. Much of this chapter includes a summation of bits and pieces regarding law enforcement and government efforts to stem organized crime. But it does no harm to tie it all together.

The Mafia still exists around Florida and throughout the world and perhaps always will, although the ethnicities have broadened greatly from Italian ancestry. Family members still get expelled or whacked if they get out of line or don't follow orders; bosses come and go as generations change. Some Mafiosi managed to leave the life of their own accord or died from natural causes; others cooperated with the government and went into the Witness Protection Program. Many of them now openly talk about their lives of crime on YouTube and other platforms or have written memoirs.

A massive impact to the existence of once powerful Mafia families is the FBI with its enormous resources to fight organized crime. Sophisticated eavesdropping, 24/7 surveillance, development of confidential informants, sharing of information with domestic and foreign intelligence agencies, aggressive investigative reporters, and the institution of laws that resulted in far longer prison sentences have put major dents in the power that the Mafia enjoyed from the 1920s to the '50s. Through the 1980s they still commanded great influence.

One element suggesting that the Mafia has seen its best days is the difference between the *Cosa Nostra* former allegiance to *omerta* compared to the situation in the last few decades. The original Mafia usually stayed away from illegal drug trafficking and officially disdained it up until the 1980s, but the lure of big money switched allegiance away from family loyalties. Prosecutions involving heavy sentences and age attrition lessened the number of old-time anti-drug hoods.

Some predict that the Mafia's future will be to continue to shrink. Others say, "Don't be naïve; that's just what the mob wants us to think."

Most certainly, the allure that originally drove Mafiosi from points north to Florida isn't nearly as powerful. We still have the sunshine and beaches, but engaging in illegal acts is far tougher when it comes to dealing with the long arm of the law. Florida police departments are much larger and more sophisticated; prosecutors and courts receive heavy media scrutiny; the average Joe nowadays, armed with a cell phone, is much more prone to expose wrongdoing or report suspicious activities. Citizens can become informants anonymously and even get rewarded for it.

I tend to agree with those who doubt the reach of today's Mafia. It well may be larger than we think, and to be sure elements from Mafia families outside the state still have representation in Florida. It's believed that the Bonanno, Gambino and Genovese families have members operating in South Florida and the Gambinos are present in Tampa as well. The Lucchese family may also have representatives operating in Tampa Bay.

Albert Joseph Facchiano, known as "Chinkie" and "The Old Man," was long a mobster in Miami with the Genovese family, and he lived to be 101—he even got indicted at age 96 and died in 2011.

It's believed that the Cuban Mafia has locked up Miami. Mexican and Russian crime families have taken root. Organized crime and corruption still reign supreme in varying levels in rural towns, where the good ol' boy networks still control local politics and business. But even that is changing as people flock to Florida, the population now over 22 million and growing. As the leadership torches are passed from one generation to the next, so is that of the Florida Mafia. Cocaine cowboys ride off into the sunset, only for new riders to occupy the stirrups.

Some things change; some never will. As long as there's money offered under the table and people with no moral compass accepting it, corruption will exist. Where corruption takes root, crime festers and grows. Now and then the federal government wins the day, and a chronology of federal agencies and congressional committees has made it tougher to get away with murder.

Some agencies preceded the dynamic expansion of Mafia families in the early 1900s, such as the IRS and Secret Service. In addition, many cities formed task forces specifically to identify and prosecute the bad guys, along with state efforts such as the Florida Department of Law Enforcement. Here are some of the significant dates regarding Mafia- and organized crime–fighting agencies and government committees:

- 1935 Federal Bureau of Investigation begins
- 1950 Senate Special Committee to Investigate Crime in Interstate Commerce (better known as the Kefauver Committee)
- 1957 United States Select Committee on Improper Activities in Labor and Management
- 1964 U.S. Senate Select Committee on Improper Activities in Labor and Management
- 1968 Gun Control Act
- 1968 Omnibus Crime Control and Safe Streets Act
- 1969 U.S. Marshals Service started
- 1970 Racketeer Influenced and Corrupt Organizations (RICO) Act
- 1972 House Select Committee on Organized Crime
- 1973 Drug Enforcement Agency originates
- 1982 Organized Crime Drug Enforcement Task Forces
- 1996 Commission on the Advancement of Federal Law Enforcement (Title 18)

While all these actions and agencies are important in fighting organized crime, several stand out. First is the U.S. Treasury Department's FBI. For more than 20 years FBI Director J. Edgar Hoover denied the existence of the American Mafia—many historians think Hoover did know it existed but in essence didn't want to admit that it was flourishing despite efforts by the FBI to curtail it; others believe the reason for his denials is that Hoover was blackmailed by the Mafia due to allegations of homosexuality.

The Kefauver Committee hearings in 1950 changed any doubt about the presence of highly organized Mafia syndicates. Even though the investigation revealed only the tip of the iceberg, it made public the Mafia's enormous influence in terms of corruption and racketeering activities. Chaired by Tennessee Senator Estes Kefauver and including four other senators— Herbert O'Conor, Charles Tobey, Lester Hunt and Alexander Wiley—the committee convened in 14 cities, including Miami and Tampa, with more than 600 witnesses testifying on a newfangled thing called television.

The hearings created a far greater public awareness of the Mafia than ever before, and Kefauver became a national sensation. The first hearing was held in downtown Miami at the federal building, with Chief Counsel

In March 1951 an estimated 30 million people watched the televised proceedings of Tennessee Senator Estes Kefauver's Special Committee on Organized Crime in Interstate Commerce. (U.S. Senate Historical Office)

Rudolph Halley heading the committee's staff. The ensuing hearings put enormous pressure on law enforcement to begin shutting down casinos operating illegally.

In addition, a huge national bookmaking syndicate based in Miami known as S&G, as we've already noted, began disintegrating due to intense pressure by former FBI agent Dan Sullivan, who at the time served as the operating director of the Crime Commission of Greater Miami. Sullivan, anti-crime crusader Mel Richard, and other Miami influencers who refused to be bought off showed the committee a chart of South Florida casinos and organized crime mobsters associated with them, the extent of which astonished everyone.

Soon thereafter, the partners in the S&G syndicate fled Miami, and casinos shut down. For the rest of the 1950s the Mafia switched its focus to casino hotels in Havana with the full support and participation of then dictator Fulgencio Batista.

Kefauver felt that the hearings didn't produce sufficient legislation to equal the magnitude of the findings, and only modest legislative measures were taken as a result of the 14 hearings. At the end of the report on the Special Committee on Organized Crime in Interstate Commerce is this statement regarding the committee's results:

> *The committee's legislative achievements were modest, at best. Kefauver favored the creation of a Federal Crime Commission, which the FBI and Department of Justice ardently opposed. The committee's second chairman, Herbert O'Conor (who took over after an exhausted Kefauver stepped down as chairman), sponsored legislation aimed at controlling illegal drugs by expanding appropriations for the Narcotics Bureau, the committee's sole legislative accomplishment.*
>
> *More important were the non-legislative results of the investigation. By bringing public opinion to bear on the problems of interstate crime, the investigation helped local and state law enforcement and elected officials to aggressively pursue criminal syndicates. The hearings clearly demonstrated that some elected officials had facilitated and profited from criminal activities. These dramatic hearings also made certain that television would play a large role in future Senate investigations.*

Kefauver wasn't the only member of Congress dogging the Mafia. Arkansas Senator John McClellan climbed into the Mafia ring in 1957 with a committee to investigate *Cosa Nostra* takeovers of labor unions. Ten years later he proposed senate bills in the 89th and 90th congressional sessions to define the Mafia and its members, reading as follows:

> *Whoever on and after the date of enactment of this Act knowingly and willfully becomes or remains a member of (1) the Mafia, or (2) any other organization having for one of its purposes the use of any interstate commerce facility in the commission of acts which are in violation of the criminal laws of the United States or any State, relating to gambling, extortion, blackmail, narcotics, prostitution, or labor-racketeering, with knowledge of the purpose of such organization, shall be guilty of a felony and upon conviction shall be imprisoned for not less than five years nor more than twenty years and may be fined not more than $20,000.*
>
> *"Mafia" means a secret society whose members are pledged and dedicated to commit unlawful acts against the United States or any State thereof in furtherance of their objective to dominate organized crime and whose operations are conducted under a secret code of terror and reprisal not only for members who fail to abide by the edicts, decrees, decisions, principles, and instructions of the society in implementation*

of this domination of organized crime, but also for those persons, not members, who represent a threat to the security of the members or the criminal operations of the society.

Bobby Kennedy used his clout as U.S. attorney general in the early 1960s to try and bust the Mafia. The irony is the allegation that Sam Giancana, the boss of the Chicago Outfit, held up the vote in Cook County and stuffed the ballot sufficiently to swing Illinois to JFK and the presidency. Some say that the mob exacted revenge by assassinating both JFK and Bobby.

In 1970 a law was enacted that made prosecutions of Mafia members much easier: the Racketeer Influenced and Corrupt Organizations (RICO) Act. Historically, mob bosses were difficult to prosecute because they seldom directly engaged in crimes and instead ordered subordinates to do so. That enabled the successful tactic of the IRS going after them for tax fraud.

Since law enforcement by then fully understood the hierarchy of a Mafia family, RICO made bosses culpable, since it was relatively easy to convince a jury that a major crime could not be carried out without the approval of members up the line. For example, if a soldier whacked someone, the feds knew that that could only be approved by the family's boss and known to the underboss, consigliere and caporegimes.

Created in 1957, the United States Select Committee on Improper Activities in Labor and Management headed by Senator John McClellan of Arkansas exposed the Mafia's influence in America's labor unions. Seated to his right is Senator Bobby Kennedy of New York. (U.S. Senate Historical Office)

In addition, RICO bundled crimes under the broad umbrella of racketeering, which includes prosecutions involving theft, fraud (mail, wire, insurance, bankruptcy), gambling, arson, drug trafficking, kidnapping, robbery, bribery, money laundering, terrorism, and of course murder. Many nuances are associated with RICO prosecutions, such as differences between criminal and civil cases, but there's no need to get into the weeds on all that.

Suffice it to say that RICO took away many of the "I don't know nuthin'" defenses by bosses. The RICO act allowed the government to confiscate assets from those convicted, such as cash, vehicles, airplanes, jewelry, real estate and other property that was often auctioned off to compensate for the government's high costs of investigating and prosecuting the cases.

EPILOGUE

As stated in the prologue, the world is fascinated about the Mafia due to its brutality, power, and colorful cast of characters. The media mantra "If it bleeds, it leads" still seems to apply in its sensationalizing of violence.

In reading about the mobsters who came to Florida to engage in criminal enterprises, we seldom think of the victims of organized crime or of the cost to our economy. Businesses figure in a certain percentage for internal and external theft, and pass that along to consumers. Arsons due to insurance fraud jack up the costs to every policyholder. Business owners trying to run successful companies are often extorted out of money by street bosses for "protection." Those who borrow shylocking money often get a broken leg or worse if payments are late. Those who dare to squeal face certain death if caught wearing a wire or outed as a rat. Bystanders often catch a bullet meant for someone else. Families of wise guys suffer when their sons, brothers or dads end up in prison.

And yet movies, books, TV series and documentaries depicting mobsters never seem to be out of vogue. The public remains captivated by the likes of Capone, Luciano, Costello, Gotti and other bad actors. Some of the dons appeared quite dapper when in the media spotlight, but none of us would want to be around when their dark sides flame to the fore.

I hope *Sunshine State Mafia* has provided a sense of history regarding some of Florida's criminal pioneers and that my personal experiences as a security consultant have resonated with you. Nothing in my book will put anyone in prison, but at the same time I dutifully researched numerous sources to attempt to depict events accurately and to separate the pepper from the fly poop. At times archives, testimonials, and court records themselves contain inconsistent or contradictory data that were difficult or impossible to corroborate. Single-person sources often engage in self-aggrandizement and stretch the truth or even fabricate individuals' escapades. I hope you appreciate that I exercised due diligence, and I hope misstated facts or incorrect assumptions are few.

I'd appreciate any comments you may care to offer. Perhaps you know a wise guy with a cool story or have a picture of a shooter at the grassy knoll. Feel free to contact me at SunshineStateMafia@gmail.com.

FAMILY LINEUPS

It's difficult to keep up-to-date on the administrations of Mafia families as arrests, convictions, retirements, or dying by violent or natural causes result in a constant flux. Law enforcement is reticent to make public what they know about current leadership of crime organizations.

What the public learns about crime administrations is often dug up by media outlets with connections to law enforcement insiders. Unfortunately, that information is sketchy and often inaccurate. By the time congressional committees publicize family organizational charts at hearings they're already dated or obsolete.

Some believe that the remnants of the Trafficante family in Tampa are now overseen by the Gambino family in NYC. The Miami mob is a conglomeration of Cuban factions rather than one organized structure, with representatives from northern Mafia families keeping fingers in the pie. Jacksonville organized crime mainly consists of many street gangs, and the isolated incidents in the Panhandle may be associated with the growing influence of the Mexican Mafia.

With that in mind, here is a probable lineup as of 2022 of bosses and underbosses, according to various sources. Note that it's sometimes difficult to discern which reports are the most current.

New York City

Bonanno Family

For the past 10 years, the boss of the Bonanno family has been Michael "The Nose" Mancuso. He'd been convicted of murder and released from prison on March 12, 2019. Joseph "Joe C" Cammarano Jr. has more or less been the acting boss since 2013. I did see a report that John Palazzolo is the underboss. The family took some major hits in 2017 and 2018 from FBI investigations that led to prison terms for many of the members.

Colombo Family

The death of Carmine "The Snake" Persico in 2019 ended his 46-year reign as boss, and his cousin Andrew "Andy Mush" Russo died in April 2022 at age 87 after serving in various roles, such as caporegime, acting boss and boss. It now appears that the acting underboss is Benjamin "Benji" Castellazzo. The major disruption in the administration of the Colombo family and multiple arrests in the last few years will make it interesting to see who takes over. Such is the quandary in keeping up-to-date with mob leadership names and titles.

Gambino Family

Following the turbulent aftermath of John "Teflon Don" Gotti, Domenico "Italian Dom" Cefalu had been the official boss, but he semi-retired in 2015. After acting boss Francesco "Franky Boy" Cali was assassinated in 2019, Peter "One Eye" Cali grabbed the reins of power, only to meet his demise in 2021. One report lists veteran Gambino hit man Lorenzo "Lore" Mannino as boss.

Genovese Family

Liborio "Barney" Bellomo became a made man in 1977 and moved up the ranks despite stints in prison for racketeering and extortion. He even reached the title of acting boss when Vincent "The Chin" Galante got pinched. His street boss is Michael "Mickey" Ragusa. Former boss Danny Leo is in prison as of this writing. In comparison to other families, the Genovese Mafia is still relatively well organized.

Lucchese Family

Taking the title as boss for the longest stretch of time is Vittorio "Vic the Terminator" Amuso. That is despite serving a life sentence since 1992 for murder and extortion. Amuso is able to run things efficiently from prison through acting boss Michael "Big Mike" DeSantis and underboss Steven "Wonderboy" Crea. It's reported that the Lucchese family is also prospering despite periodic busts that take down various members.

Other Cities

Bruno Family, Philadelphia

The very colorful Joseph "Skinny Joey" Merlino is covered in the Palm Beach chapter. He's been the Philly boss for over 23 years, following in the footsteps of his father (Chuckie) as Nicky Scarfo's underboss. Merlino's underboss has been Michael "Mikey Lance" Lancelotti, who became indicted by the FBI in 2020 when he was recorded during a ceremony in the making of a new member and also discussing family business. However, one report indicates Merlino may have already passed the baton and hopefully it's true.

DeLaurentis/Cataudella, Chicago

Salvatore "Solly" DeLaurentis has been boss since 2014 after John "No Nose" DeFronzo retired. Though in his 80s, DeLaurentis is considered a capable don who favors mending fences between rival factions rather than indulging in gangland wars. Street boss Albert "Albie the Falcon" runs day-to-day affairs and is expected to take over when DeLaurentis retires or passes. Underboss is Salvatore "Sammy Cards" Cataudella. Although the family members aren't as public as in the flashy days of Al Capone and Sam Giancana, they're still active and prefer the lower profile.

Magaddino Family, Buffalo

The boss of Buffalo is Joseph "Big Joe" Todaro Jr. While not as infamous as the NYC families, the Buffalo family has been around for over 100 years. In the 1980s Todaro Sr. ruled the family. Underboss is Domenico Violi, whose primary role seems to be supervising the family's Canadian crime interests. The Magaddino family is still actively involved in various racketeering enterprises while maintaining legit businesses.

Patriarca Family, New England

Based in Rhode Island, the family oversees criminal activities in several New England states. Carmen "The Cheese Man" DiNunzio is a Bostonian and got his nickname when owning a cheese store. He reportedly weighs around 400 pounds. DiNunzio previously served as underboss, as did his brother Anthony before him, and in 2016 Carmen became boss when former boss Peter Limone died. Matthew "Good Looking Matty" Gugliemetti is the underboss.

Tocco/Giacalone, Detroit

Also known as the Detroit Partnership, the family was run by longtime boss Giacomo Tocco, who died in 2014, whereupon Jackie "The Kid" Giacalone became boss. He hails from a family tradition of Mafia involvement, his father and uncle having served as capos. Besides criminal activities, the family invests in legit businesses and as a relatively small organization stays off the radar screen. Extortion, illegal drugs and loansharking are their forte.

During the McClellan hearings in the mid-1960s, family charts caused quite a stir. To view a selection of Mafia family charts from the heyday of the mob, visit www.gangrule.com.

MAFIOSI DOMICILES

For those intent on driving by residences of former Mafia members who lived full- or part-time in Florida, keep in mind that some of these addresses are decades old. They may not exist anymore, or don't look as they did when mobsters inhabited them, or may now be occupied by people who have nothing to do with organized crime.

All the Trafficante family members lived in the Tampa Bay area, although Santo Jr. also maintained a residence in Miami. Family members listed here with nicknames in parentheses rather than quote marks lived in northern states and also maintained Florida residences, with most in South Florida.

Fort Lauderdale to West Palm Beach

Gerardo (Jerry) Catena—2100 Coconut Road, Boca Raton
Frank Gagliardi—2180 N.E. 63 Court, Fort Lauderdale
Ettore (Terry) Zappi—2764 17th Street, Fort Lauderdale

Hallandale and Hollywood

Anthony (Sumac) Accetturo Sr.—5000 Grant Street, Hollywood Hills
Vincent (Jimmy Blue Eyes) Alo—1248 Monroe Street, Hollywood
Sebastiano (Buster) Aloi—1720 Moffitt Street, Hollywood
Joseph (Demus) Covello—707 Diplomat Parkway, Hallandale
Jabob (Jake) Lansky—1146 Harrison Street, Hollywood
Meyer (The Genius, The Mob's Accountant, The Little Man) Lansky—612 Hibiscus Dr., Hallandale; 5255 Collins Avenue, Miami Beach; 5001 Collins Avenue, Miami Beach
Joseph (Joey Narrow) Laratro—543 Palm Drive, Hallandale
Alfonzo (Don Alfonso) Marzano—729 N.E. Third Street, Hallandale

Gaetano (Tony Gobels) Ricci—1332 Van Buren Street, Hollywood

George (Georgie Blair) Smurra—1404 Plunket Street, Hollywood

Miami Area

(See also Meyer Lansky under Hallandale for his two Miami addresses)

Dominick (Cokey Dom) Alongi—520 N.E. 38 Street, Miami

Anthony (Tony the Enforcer) Altamura—1075 N.E. 88 Street, Miami

Frank Amato—1160 N.E. 137 Street, Miami

Salvatore (Sal the Sailor) Ciccone—10225 Collins Avenue, Bal Harbour

Frank (Big Frankie) Cocchiaro—7545 Bounty Road, North Bay Village

Ettore (Little Eddie) Coco—550 N.W. 123 Street, Miami

Mike (Trigger Mike) Coppola—4431 Alton Road, Miami Beach

William (Willy the Tile Maker) Dara—15301 N.E. 6 Avenue,

Simone (Sam the Plumber) DeCavalcante—5601 Collins Avenue, Miami

Frankie (Frankie Dio) Dioguardi—1021 N.E. 162 Street, No. Miami Beach

Pasquale (Little Patsy) Erra—5609 N.W. 7 Avenue, Miami; 3720 Chase
    Avenue, Miami Beach

James (Jimmy Black) Falco—6905 Willow Lane, Miami Lakes

North Miami

Alfredo (Freddy Red Shirt) Felice—1770 Normandie Drive, Miami Beach;
    7710 Beachview Drive, North Bay Village

Joseph (Joe Scootch) Indelicato—1900 S. Treasure Drive, North Bay Vil-
    lage

Joseph (Georgie Blue Eyes) Martinelli—4480 Michigan Street, Miami
    Beach

John (Johnny Irish) Matera—1943 N.E. 175 Street, Miami Beach

George (Georgie the Hook) Nobile—1021 N.E. 162 Street, N. Miami Beach

Vincent (Jimmy Dee) Palmisano—791 N.E. 154 Street, North Miami

Anthony (Tony Plate) Plata—1230 101 Street, Bay Harbour

Anthony (Little Pussy) Russo—1583 N.E. 109 Street, Miami

Anthony (Fat Tony) Salerno—1041 Venetian Drive, Miami Beach

Santo Trafficante Jr.—740 N.E. 155 Street, North Miami

ACKNOWLEDGMENTS

Big thanks to the University Press of Florida for recognizing the potential for *Sunshine State Mafia*. UPF published my first book a dozen years ago and the experience with them then and ever since has been very rewarding.

An author's success and hidden ace is a talented editor who provides invaluable insights, suggestions, and criticisms that elevate the final product. In that vein, I offer a zillion thanks to Sian Hunter, my acquisitions editor at UPF. She's endured my eccentricities with aplomb and is the essence of a delightful collaborator. Carlynn Crosby, UPF's acquisitions coordinator, has been another huge asset in the desire to put out a professional and accurate product. Sally Antrobus did a superb job of proofreading, and managing editor Marthe Walters ably moved the book through all the editorial stages. That's a dream team you want in your corner.

I also give constant hugs and kisses to wife Kelly Kelly—that's really her name, and yes, she married me anyway!—whose thoughtful advice and tolerance are never taken for granted. Kelly also applied her artistic talents by offering design suggestions for the book cover and in devising the Mafia family chart in the first chapter.

No historical work can be written without prior research and writings by authors of books, newspaper and magazine articles, websites, blogs and newsletters. Many others lent a hand with images (some being family archives never before published) and offered valuable suggestions, especially acclaimed organized crime authors Scott Deitche and Avi Bash.

The following folks and organizations deserve a gold mine for their input to make *Sunshine State Mafia* a special historical work: Stu Apte, Capt. Skip Bradeen, Dean Butler, Jessica Cotsonas, Roben Farzad, Natalia Crujeiras, the FBI, Carl Fismer, Florida Department of Corrections, Florida Memory, Jack Hexter, my daughter Lynn and son Michael Kelly, Rodney Kite-Powell, Katrina Kochneva, the Library of Congress, Monroe County Public Libraries/Florida Keys History Center, Tom Peeling, Quincy Perkins, Al Pflueger, Carole Russo, Kevin Russo, Jeremy Salloum,

David Sloan, Breana Sowers, Tampa Bay History Center, The Other Guy at the ButtonGuysoftheNewYorkMafia.com, Capt. Earle Waters, and Zuma Press. For anyone I've left out, a million mea culpas.

To those who did cross the line into organized crime and for whatever motivation turned their lives around, I hope one day to shake your hand and hear your stories. The last perfect person died over 2,000 years ago, so it's never too late to start down a more righteous path. You might not be as rich or as feared as a wise guy, but you'll have gained something more priceless: peace of mind for yourself and family.

GLOSSARY

Here is a partial list of oft-used Mafia terms and definitions:

Administration – The top level of a family composed of the boss, underboss and consigliere.

Apprenticeship – A period of time between being proposed by a made man and being made, wherein the apprentice—usually called a recruit—must carry out whatever orders he's told and put his Mafia family before all other priorities.

Associate – The lowest-ranking member of a family who is not a made man due to heritage, reputation or other factors.

Bleach job – Also known as spring cleaning, it's altering the scene of a murder not performed in public.

Buckwheat – Can refer to stripping someone's authority or committing a murder in a slow and torturous manner.

Buttonman – A made man who's often a hit man.

Buy him a hat – To bribe a cop or a cop on the take.

Canary – Same as a rat, someone who sings to the authorities.

Carry the can – Taking the blame for someone else's crime.

CI – Confidential informant.

Clip – To kill; a whack; to off; a hit.

Code of silence – Known as *omerta,* it's part of a ritual when becoming a made man who pledges to never be a rat. Original members of *La Cosa Nostra* strictly observed this code of silence, but it has become more commonly breached.

Comare – Also called a goomah; both words refer to a mistress.

Commission – A governing body formed by Lucky Luciano in 1931 originally consisting of representatives—usually the bosses—of the five NYC families and the four families outside NYC. Before a made member could be murdered, the Commission would have to give its approval. The Commission allowed the Mafia to pool resources, mediate conflicts, apportion territories, control unions and share bribed politicians, journalists and members of law enforcement.

Connected guy – An associate.

Crew – A team of made men and sometimes associates, usually under the direction of a capo.

Cosine – A man hoping to become made.

Don – Though a term seldom used except in movies or books, he's a family boss.

Earner – One who generates money from racketeering and legitimate businesses for himself and his Mafia family.

Eats alone – As in "he eats alone," it's a euphemism for someone who doesn't share earnings or is an independent criminal.

Family business – To take part in, and be a member of, the criminal underworld.

Federales – Federal agents such as those in the Federal Bureau of Investigation (FBI), Drug Enforcement Agency (DEA), and the Bureau of Alcohol, Tobacco and Firearms (ATF).

Garbage business or biz – Also known as "waste management business," a veiled reference to those involved in organized crime, as in "he's in the garbage biz."

Guzzling – Making a bet and then not paying the bookmaker if you lose.

Heat – The unwanted attention of law enforcement.

Heavy – Also called packing, it means one who's armed, as in "I'm heavy."

Hit man – A contract killer, usually a made man or an associate who's part of a crew.

Juice – Also known as vigorish, vig or shy, the interest paid to a loan shark in addition to the amount borrowed.

Kefauver Committee – A U.S. Senate committee, created in 1950 and run by Sen. Estes Kefauver, that exposed Mafia-run gambling enterprises in Florida and elsewhere.

La Cosa Nostra – Italian for "Our thing" or "This Thing of Ours."

Lam – To go on the run and into hiding to prevent being arrested or whacked.

Lawyer up – Hiring a lawyer when pinched so as not to cooperate or provide a statement.

Made man – A man of full or part Italian descent who qualifies per existing Mafia criteria to become a member of a family.

Mafia – A general term for an Italian organized crime family, although it's come to be broadly used with other ethnicities, such as the Irish Mafia or Mexican Mafia.

Mafiosi – Plural reference to two or more Mafia members.

Mafioso – Singular reference to a Mafia member.

Making the Bones – An ordered murder that's required to become a made man.

Muscle – A tough guy or guys who provide security and enforce a family's decisions, but who also can be earners.

Order – What a proposed or made man is told to do and expected to do, such as carrying out a hit or a rough up.

Paying tribute – Giving the boss a cut of the take, also known as kicking up to the boss.

Pinched – Being arrested.

Pledge – The definition of a man who's been proposed.

Points – A percentage of money passed to a boss or family that is obtained legally or illegally by other families, such as sharing a portion of a union contract.

Proposed – Being proposed is when a made man recommends someone—usually but not always an associate—to be considered a member of a Mafia family.

Rat – Short for ratfink, one who snitches or squeals after being pinched.

Recruitment period – The time after being proposed to see if he's worthy of becoming made, which can take months or years.

Rod – A handgun, also called a heater or a piece.

Rough up – Also called knee busting, arm twisting or mock execution, it's beating someone up for the purpose of intimidation, retribution, or money owed.

Sending a message – Doing something to a murdered body to let the police or a rival know the purpose of it, such as a bullet through the mouth to designate a rat.

Shakedown – To blackmail a person or business, to collect money, or to give someone a scare.

Shylocking – A loan shark operation.

Sit down – A meeting usually arranged between bosses, under bosses or caporegimes to agree on courses of action or to negotiate a dispute, particularly when it involves an intent to whack someone.

Soldier or soldato – A made man, the level between an associate and a caporegime.

Street boss – A term often used to describe a family's caporegime.

Street guy – One who's experienced in dealing with day-to-day situations on the streets and neighborhoods, also known as being street wise. He can be an earner and gain enough respect to move up the ladder in authority.

Sucker – A term often used by made men in reference to an associate.

Taking the fifth – Exercising one's right under the Fifth Amendment to the U.S. Constitution, whereby someone is not forced to testify against himself or herself.

Tax – To take a percentage of someone's earnings.

The Outfit – Can be a reference to any family but commonly a reference to the Chicago Outfit. The Chicago Outfit was first run by Capone and later Frank Nitti, Anthony Accardo and Sam Giancana. The Outfit had a seat on the Commission and initially was the main family to back and operate Las Vegas casinos, earning millions in skim money.

The Program – The Federal Witness Protection Program provided to someone when arrested in exchange for testifying. The witness is given a new identity and moved (along with his immediate family if married) to an undisclosed location.

Whack – To murder, hit, pop, eliminate, off, rub out, kill.

Wise guy – A made member of the Mafia.

BIBLIOGRAPHY

I could list hundreds of sources available online that I researched, an advantage in terms of time and travel that authors nowadays enjoy. However, the following links are examples that I found particularly interesting and informative.

Websites/Articles

AboutTheMafia.com

A&E's American Justice Mafia episodes, Current Mafia Bosses in 2022

ButtonGuysoftheNewYorkMafia.com

crimehistoryinc.org (Hollywood, FL)

crimetoursmuseum.com (Hollywood, FL)

historymiami.org (Miami)

J. Coletti's Racket Reviews (series)

miaminewtimes.com/arts/a-guide-to-al-capones-miami-landmarks-11630366 (Capone, Miami)

modisarchitects.com/2017/05/new-museum-capture-little-havanas-history/(Miami)

search.library.wisc.edu/database/UWI60374 (FBI Surveillance in Florida and Cuba of Lansky and Santo Trafficante Jr.)

tampabay.com/archive/1991/05/05/who-are-tampa-s-new-mob-leaders/ (Old list of Tampa Mafia succession)

thenewyorkmafia.com (highly recommended)

thrillist.com/travel/nation/gangster-museum-of-america-hot-springs-arkansas (Arkansas)

tulsaworld.com/archive/the-russian-mafia-invades-florida/article_0ce5fcc3-5ba2-51a3-a2d9-8b1e05e5b826.html (Russian Mafia in Florida)

upi.com/Archives/1988/04/22/FBI-agent-Life-in-the-mob-a-boring-money-grubbing-grind/5189577684800/ (Joe Pistone, a.k.a. Donny Brasco, NYC FBI undercover agent)

vault.fbi.gov/reading-room-index, https://mafiahistory.us/maf-kef.html (Kefauver hearings)

YouTube Videos, Documentaries (Links and Suggested Searches):

Michael Franzese (Yahoo channel series)
Salvatore "Sammy the Bull" Gravano (Yahoo channel series)
youtube.com/watch?v=yY2XikoFxKI
youtube.com/watch?v=-bhtBukYHEs

Books

Bash, Avi. *Organized Crime in Miami*. Mount Pleasant, SC: Arcadia Publishing, 2016.

Chepesiuk, Ron. *Gangsters of Miami: True Tales of Mobsters, Gamblers, Hit Men, Con Men and Gang Bangers from the Magic City*. Fort Lee, NJ: Barricade Books, 2010.

Deitche, Scott. *Cigar City Mafia: A Complete History of the Tampa Underworld*. Fort Lee, NJ: Barricade Books, 2004.

English, T. J. *The Corporation: An Epic Story of the Cuban American Underworld*. New York: HarperCollins, 2018.

English, T. J. *Havana Nocturne: How the Mob Owned Cuba . . . and Then Lost It to the Revolution*. New York: HarperCollins, 2007.

Ling, Sally. *Al Capone's Miami: Paradise or Purgatory?* Deerfield Beach, FL: Flamingo Press, 2015.

Russo, Carole. *Me and Jimmy Blue Eyes*. Red Penguin Books, 2020.

Zimmerman, Stan. *A History of Smuggling in Florida*. Mount Pleasant, SC: History Press, 2006.

INDEX

DOUG KELLY is the award-winning author of *Florida's Fishing Legends and Pioneers*; *Alaska's Greatest Outdoor Legends*; and *Dirty Trickster, Corporate Spy*. A veteran outdoors and travel writer, he's visited 72 countries and served on Florida and federal fisheries and wildlife management advisory councils. Kelly served as a staff editor of national magazines and for over five years has co-hosted a weekly radio show in Tampa Bay.

HISTORY/TRUE CRIME/ORGANIZED CRIME

"Kelly gives a broad view of organized crime in Florida, interspersed with his own personal anecdotes, highlighting the unique and often crazier-than-fiction story of organized crime in the Sunshine State."—**Scott M. Deitche**, author of *Cigar City Mafia: A Complete History of the Tampa Underworld*

"A fascinating and fresh look at infamous gangsters and criminals who lived and operated throughout Florida. Kelly's varied business ventures and hobbies often landed him directly among the characters depicted throughout the book, and while some readers may find many of the names familiar, it's Kelly's engrossing firsthand accounts that set this book apart from others."—**Avi Bash**, author of *Organized Crime in Miami*

A vivid, wild ride through a century of Mafia lore, this book tells stories of organized crime rings that have settled in Florida and made the state their base of operations for bootlegging, gambling, extortion, money laundering, and drug running. *Sunshine State Mafia* divulges the hidden history of the mob from the Keys to Pensacola and Jacksonville.

Featuring Al Capone and crime rings in Miami and South Florida, the Trafficante family in Tampa, Harlan Blackburn and his gambling empire in Orlando, and many more individuals both infamous and little known, this book explains how and why mob bosses from northern states came to Florida in the early 1900s—they saw the state as a respite from cold weather and a good place to evade law enforcement. The cast of characters in these stories includes cops, sheriffs, prosecutors, judges, and politicians who took bribes or even conspired with criminals.

Doug Kelly offers never-before-told information from newly released files, interviews with retired police and FBI agents, and his own career as a security consultant during the Cocaine Cowboys era. Kelly's line of work involved brushes with criminal elements and notorious characters, which he recounts here. He also defines roles within Mafia families, discusses how changes in policing have impacted the patterns of criminal organizations, and talks about what distinguishes the Mafia from other groups.

The first book to survey the origins and activities of the Mafia across Florida, *Sunshine State Mafia* will surprise readers with its insights into the influence of organized crime in the history of the state's small towns and cities.

Doug Kelly is a freelance writer and editor, as well as a licensed private investigator and security consultant. He is the author of *Dirty Trickster, Corporate Spy: A Watergate Saboteur Switches from Disrupting Campaigns to Spying on Employees*; *Alaska's Greatest Outdoor Legends: Colorful Characters Who Built the Fishing and Hunting Industries*; and *Florida's Fishing Legends and Pioneers*.

Front: top, left to right, Edward R. "Colonel" Bradley (floridamemory .com); Alphonse "Scarface" Capone's mug shot, 1939 (Federal Bureau of Investigation); Meyer Lansky (Federal Bureau of Investigation); *bottom*, bolita balls and tickets (Tampa Bay History Center).

UNIVERSITY PRESS OF FLORIDA
http://upress.ufl.edu

ISBN 978-0-8130-8048-2 $28.00